# Power Tools at Home

Harold King

INDEPENDENT TELEVISION BOOKS LTD, LONDON

**INDEPENDENT TELEVISION BOOKS LTD, LONDON**
247 Tottenham Court Road
London W1P 0AU




ISBN: 0 900 72738 1

*Research:*
Elizabeth King

*Technical assistance:*
Black & Decker Ltd, Gordon Stephens

*Technical consultant:*
Ronald Kidd

*Photography:*
Nelson Hargreaves, Robert Lock;
additional photography Ray Thatcher

*Design and layout:*
Tri-Art

Printed in Great Britain by Jarrold and Sons Ltd., Norwich




Power tools and related products used to illustrate this book were, with
few exceptions, from the range produced by Black & Decker Ltd. The
author and publishers wish to acknowledge the assistance received from
that company's Home User, Accessory and Service Divisions.

Dowelling jig by Record Tools Ltd, mimic profile former by Copydex Ltd.

# Contents

# The powerhouse

**Power tools and attachments**

An electric power drill is a basic 'power house', enabling you to speed up the many basic jobs of home repair and improvement. A versatile tool, it can accept a whole range of attachments and accessories, adding a great deal of built-in skill and precision when tackling a host of jobs, from simple fixings and drilling into a range of materials to time-consuming jobs such as carpentry.

The aim of this book is to introduce you to the wide-ranging members of the power tool family, and its attachments and accessories, which can be helpful in doing so many jobs around the house.

With its built-in strength, the power tool need not be a commodity solely of the *man* of the home; women can now take a hand in tackling 'heavy' jobs, too.

Though power tools take much of the hard work out of jobs around the home, it is important to choose the right tool for the job. The rule is to buy the best you can afford, as the more expensive tools will provide the greatest versatility and be equal to the widest range of jobs.

Often, a drill is found fault with when its limitations have been ignored. A modest, single-speed power drill cannot be expected to drill large, deep holes in concrete surfaces — something it is too often called on to do — and may be quickly damaged if it is forced to operate beyond its working capacity. A single-speed drill can do most jobs around the home, however, except for drilling in masonry and concrete.

Power tools consist of a compact electric motor encased in a shell, usually made of light-weight, high-impact plastic such as Marynal. Many modern tools are double-insulated for safety. Other than in a few cases, such as certain hedge trimmers, power tools work from the mains, connected by a cable led out through the base of the drill to a suitable plug into a power point.

The compact, modern power drill has a pistol grip, containing a 'trigger' or button, which has to be pressed to start the drill. This button is spring-loaded to release and shut off the motor when pressure is relaxed — a safety factor — though on many tools the button can be locked to the 'on' position for continuous operation. Some-times the lock device is incorporated in the drill trigger; in other cases a small button beside the trigger has to be depressed to lock the drill for continuous running.

The 'business end' of the drill contains a chuck, which can be opened or closed by means of a revolving clamp inside the chuck jaws, to grip a fitment. Chucks are available in a range of sizes — 6mm, 8mm, 10mm and 13mm are the most usual ones. The chuck size indicates the maximum size of shank of drill or fitment that can be accommodated.

On many drills, the chuck can be un-screwed and removed so that screwed fitments can be attached straight into the drill spindle. This represents a more satisfactory and firm fixing for many fitments — other than twist drills and paint stirrers, which clamp into the jaws of the chuck. When putting an accessory into the spindle, fit a fibre washer to the thread as this prevents the metal from locking.

The chuck clamps shut with a chuck key, which fits into any one of three holes on the chuck and is twisted to lock or unlock. Chuck keys are easily lost or mislaid. On some drills a clip is provided to attach the key, but it is a good idea to keep the key in a regular place — and unfailingly to return it after use. Or you can attach the key to the drill cable with a piece of wire.

Most power tool motors develop around 370W ($\frac{1}{2}$hp) in power and are cooled by a fan. Slots around the drill allow cooling air to enter; these must be kept free from dust

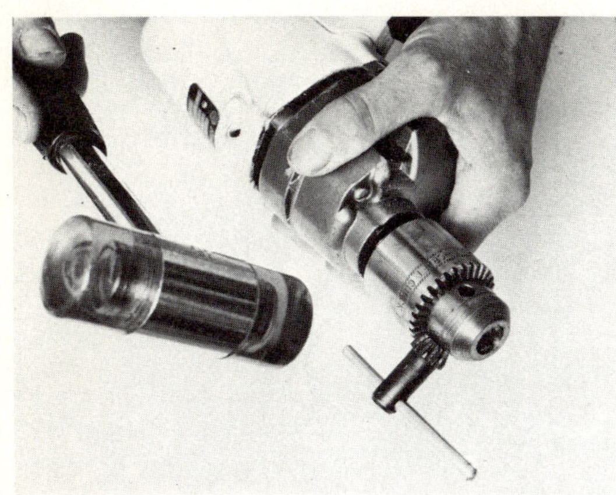

*To remove the chuck, insert the chuck key, then give it a smart hammer tap*

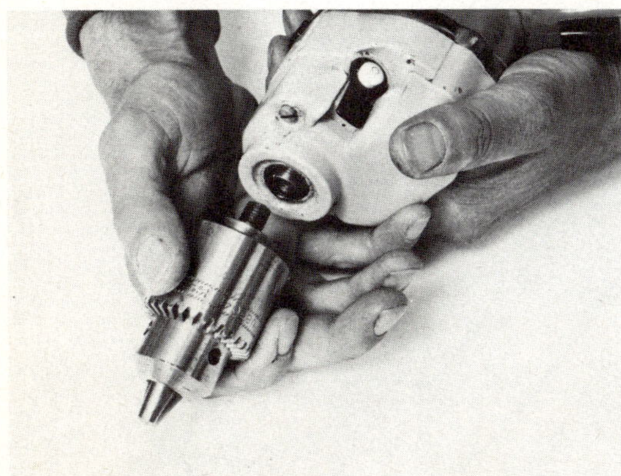

*Once the chuck has been loosened, it can easily be unscrewed by hand*

and should not be covered when in use, or the drill motor may overheat.

When the drill is switched on, current passes to the field coils, and then to the armature, via carbon brushes and the commutator. The diagram (page 6) shows the constituent parts of a power drill — the heart of the power tool workshop.

The armature of most tools has a mainshaft speed of 20–30,000 revolutions per minute (rpm), geared down to revolve at about 3000 rpm, which increases the driving force or 'torque'. The speed of the chuck is the no-load condition: when under load, it slows slightly.

Drills may be single-speed, running at up to 3000 rpm, or capable of operating at two or more speeds. Drills incorporating a slow speed — up to 1000 rpm — are essential for drilling into hard surfaces. Four-speed drills have a choice of speeds from about 600 rpm up to 3000 rpm. These possess the basic high speed and low speed plus two intermediate speeds, which are adjustable on the drill trigger.

When using a two-speed drill, do not change speed while it is running, as this may damage the gearing. Switch off and allow the drill to stop. Change speed and continue.

Variable-speed drills may be infinitely varied between low and high speeds by means of built-in electronic control. Hammer drills have an impact attachment — very useful for drilling into hard surfaces — using a special drill bit. The hammer device can be switched out for conventional drilling.

The rotary percussion device vibrates some 20,000 tiny impacts per minute, chipping into hard surfaces and facilitating penetration. The hammer device is incorporated in some two-speed, four-speed and variable-speed drills.

A single-speed tool can be converted to two-speed use by an attachment; a hammer attachment can also be readily

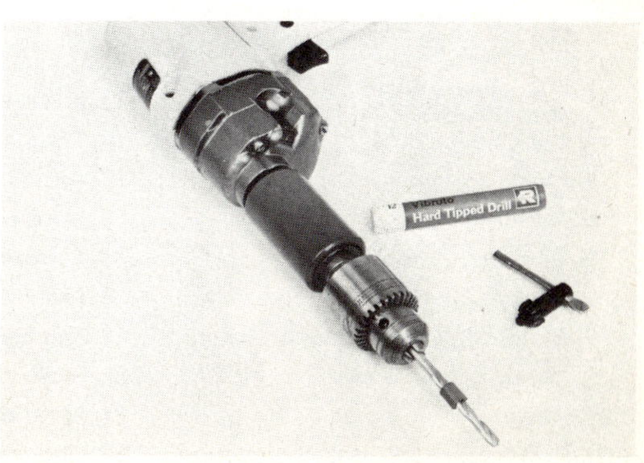

*Hammer attachment fits to a drill*

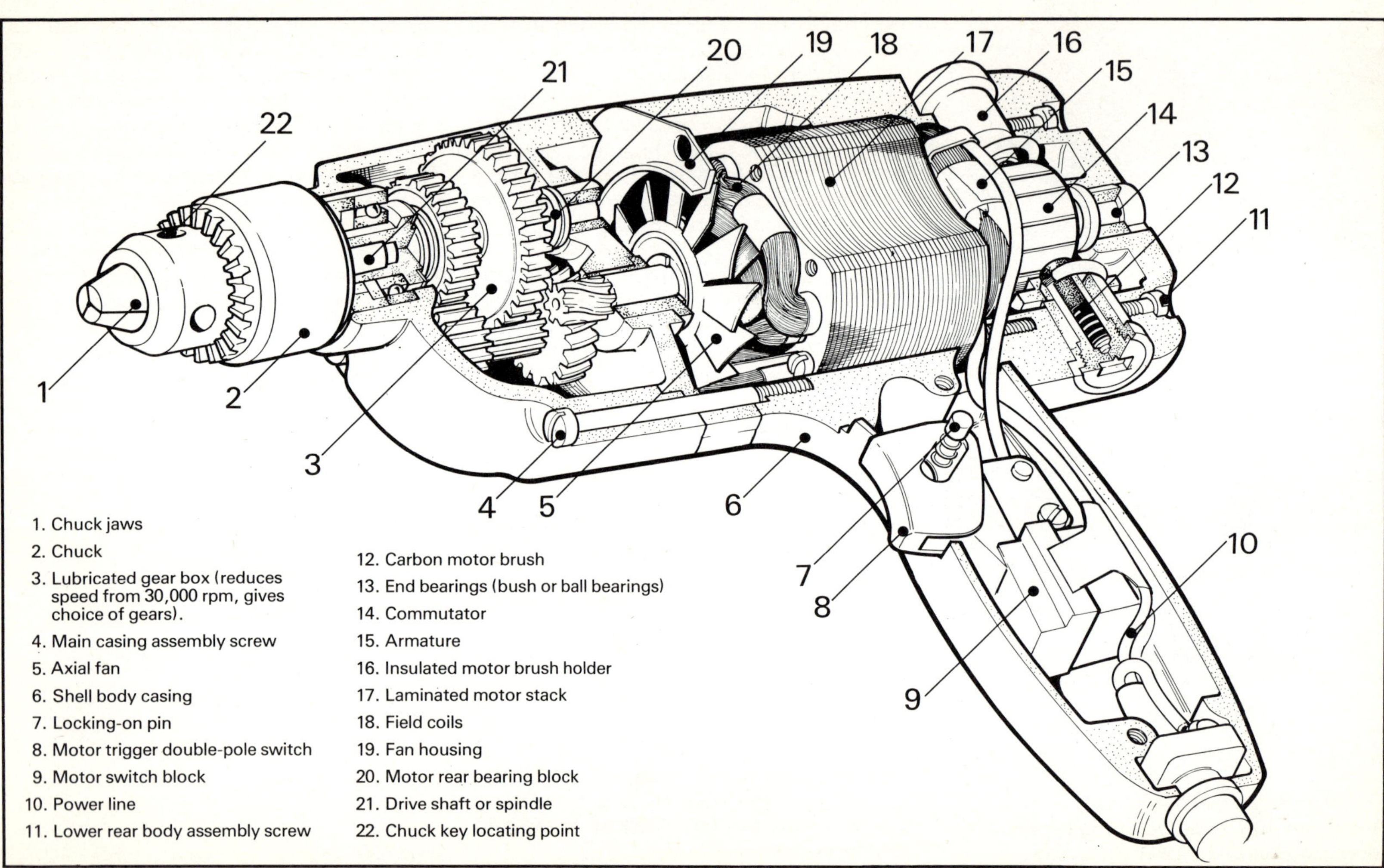

1. Chuck jaws
2. Chuck
3. Lubricated gear box (reduces speed from 30,000 rpm, gives choice of gears).
4. Main casing assembly screw
5. Axial fan
6. Shell body casing
7. Locking-on pin
8. Motor trigger double-pole switch
9. Motor switch block
10. Power line
11. Lower rear body assembly screw
12. Carbon motor brush
13. End bearings (bush or ball bearings)
14. Commutator
15. Armature
16. Insulated motor brush holder
17. Laminated motor stack
18. Field coils
19. Fan housing
20. Motor rear bearing block
21. Drive shaft or spindle
22. Chuck key locating point

fitted to a standard drill. However, it is more economical to buy a drill incorporating the features you require, rather than gradually to buy attachments for a power tool, as the cost of these will add up to more than a drill with the built-in facilities.

In choosing a drill, look ahead and consider the uses you might have in the future, rather than what you want the drill for at the time of purchase. It is a good idea to buy a budget-priced extra drill and keep this solely for attachments. This can save you a lot of time and will speed up your work.

Attachments convert a power drill into a variety of other tools, such as the circular saw, orbital or finishing sander, hedge cutter, jig or power saw and bench grinder.

A purpose-designed unit, called an 'integral' tool, is made to do one job — such as sawing or finish-sanding. The integral tool saves time, for you do not have to stop work to fit the bits and pieces of attachments to the drill before carrying on; and because the unit is purpose-designed it usually does the job better than attachments to a power drill.

**Choosing power tools**
A power drill is a modest investment in terms of its versatility and time-saving abilities, but by extending your power tool workshop you must expect to run into a fairly moderate capital outlay.

It is therefore a good idea to draw up a budget-buying plan for building up your power tool kit. By buying an attachment or accessory each week or month, your kit will grow surprisingly quickly.

Make a list of the jobs you may wish to tackle around the house — both improvements and routine maintenance — and relate the uses of power equipment to these.

You should start with a power drill, useful mainly for fixing — that is drilling holes — one of the jobs you are most likely to want to do. Remember, however, that fast-speed single-speed drills are not generally suitable for drilling into hard wall surfaces.

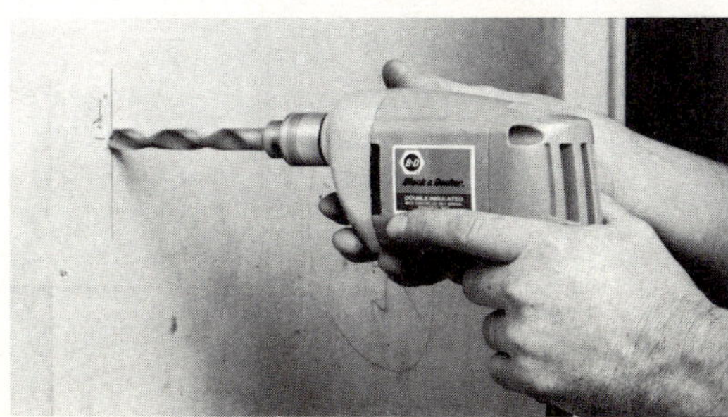

*Budget-priced drill is useful extra*

The power saw, either an attachment or, preferably, an integral unit, should be next on your shopping list, for its capabilities range from sawing timber to cutting floorboards and many jobs in between.

A saw bench is an investment that will make a power circular saw even more versatile. Smoothing and finishing are other common jobs, and a finishing or orbital sander or attachment enables you to provide a high-grade finish on a variety of surfaces.

The disc-sanding pad is a useful attachment for generally smoothing down a surface. With other attachments, a whole range of specialized cutting jobs can be tackled in high-grade woodworking.

A power workshop, accessories and attachments save much hard work and add precision in a host of jobs

This selection of Black & Decker power tools, though not intended to be comprehensive, represents a wide range with which you could tackle almost any home repair or improvement job.

1.  D720 two-speed drill

2.  Vertical drill stand (with above drill) and drill vice

3.  D500N single-speed drill

4.  Horizontal drill stand

5.  V850 two-speed drill

6.  Horizontal stand and sanding and sharpening face-plate

7.  Wood-turning lathe (with drill and horizontal stand)

8.  Circular-saw blade

9.  Sanding plate (used on sanding and sharpening table and on lathe for face-plate turning)

10. Saw bench

11. Saw attachment fitted to D500N drill mounted in bench

12. Jig-saw attachment

13. Bench grinder

14. Router

15. Drill-bit sharpener

16. Finishing (orbital) sander

17. Airless spray gun

18. Milling table (used with vertical drill stand)

19. Portable integral saw

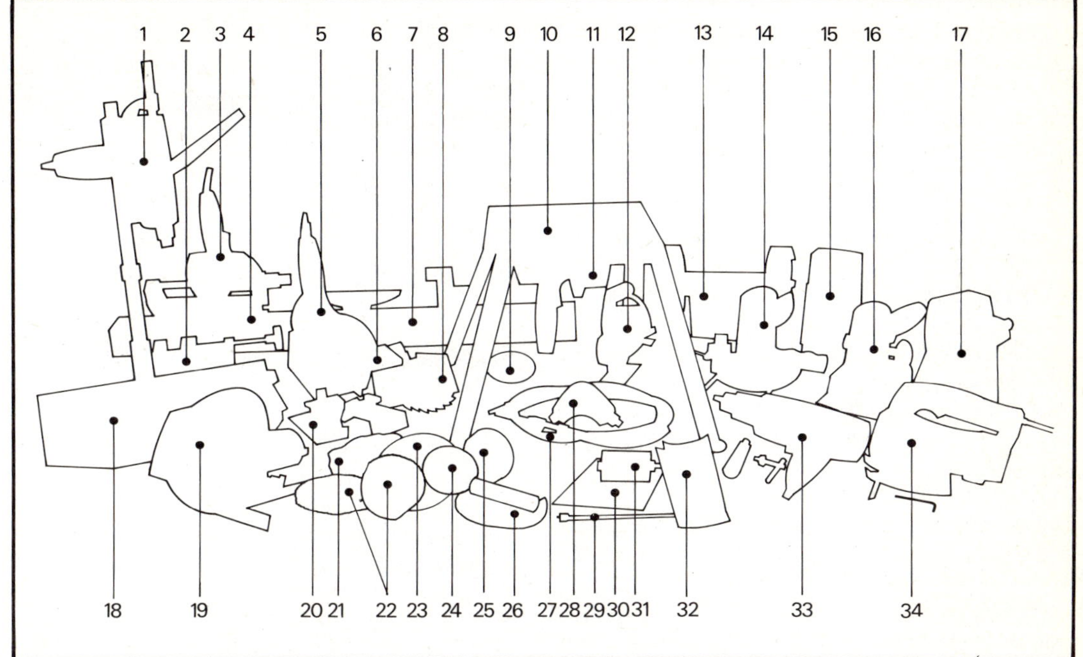

20. Comb-jointing attachment (uses saw blade and horizontal drill stand)

21. Lambswool polishing bonnet

22. Wire wheel and wire cup brush attachments

23. Rubber backing pad (sanding and polishing)

24. Rag buff (polishing)

25. Grinding wheel with arbor (fits to drill on horizontal stand or bench grinder)

26. Sanding discs and cement (latter for face-plate fixing)

27. Flexible drive (rotary tool in chuck)

28. Right-angle speed changer

29. Wood power bit

30. Set of rotary tools

31. Impact hammer attachment

32. Sanding sheets (finishing sander)

33. V870 variable-speed hammer drill (with chuck key and side handle)

34. Integral jig saw (power saw)

# Bits – and other pieces

The basic power drill, with the correct bit, is designed to drill holes accurately and quickly in a wide variety of materials – but you must observe the correct speed and use a suitable drill piece. The size of the chuck indicates the maximum size of shank of the bit that can fit into the chuck.

Drill bits for power drills have rounded shanks to fit into the chuck. Never use hand-tool bits – these have squared shanks and the jaws will not grip the shank properly; the bit could slip in use and be dangerous. A power drill harnesses considerable 'torque' or driving force and the chuck is turning very fast, even at a slow speed.

Twist bits possess heads no wider than the shank; average domestic bits are made in sizes of from 2mm up to 13mm and sometimes beyond, and can be used to drill a wide range of materials. There are two choices of steel for twist drills – carbon or high-speed. High-speed steel is best for general use, as this has a much better life than carbon steel, which blunts very quickly.

For cutting larger holes, above 13mm, for metal or other hard materials other than masonry, a hole saw is used. Hole saws, also called trepanning bits, enable holes of up to 100mm in diameter to be drilled,

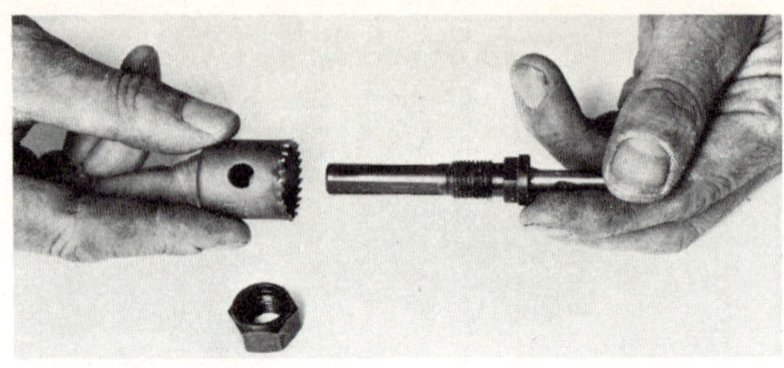

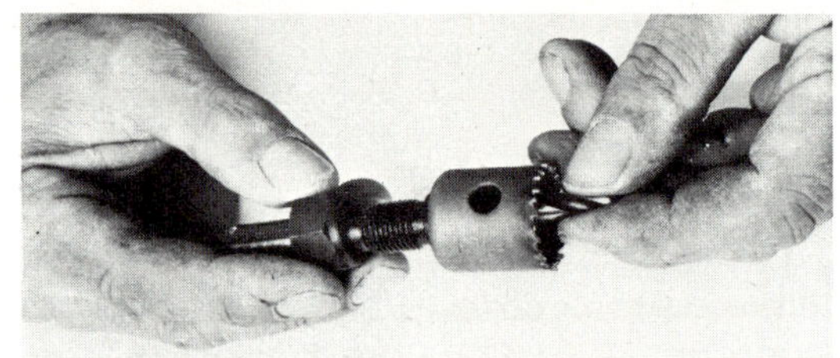

*The hole saw, in a range of sizes, is used mainly to make holes on electrical and plumbing work*

up to a depth of 50mm in timber. The maximum thickness of metal you can cut with a hole saw is 5mm.

Hole saws consist of a revolving, toothed ring, which fits over a centre drill piece or mandrel. The saw bodies are interchangeable and are available in a range of sizes. They can be used for cutting holes for plumbing and electrical work.

For timber, large drills called augers, with heads larger than the shank, are used.

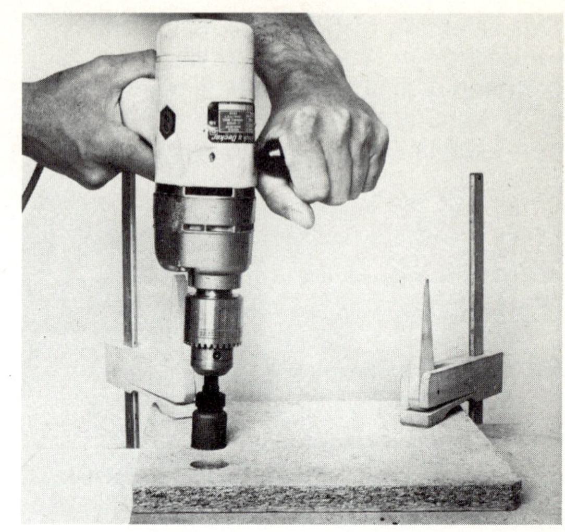

*This fits on to a centre drill bit or mandrel; can be hand-held or used in a bench stand*

These allow holes of up to about twice the size of the chuck to be drilled.

Augers have large spirals to remove the waste from the hole in wood, with a centre spike or spur to start the hole accurately. Flat bits, sometimes called spade bits, are other larger drill pieces. These have a centre spike and two wide cutters. As the name suggests, the body of the bit is spade-shaped.

Forstner bits, which make neat, flat-bottomed holes, must be used only with the drill fitted in a drill stand. These holes need cleaning out more frequently than those made with an auger.

Larger holes, up to 32mm in diameter, can be drilled with flat bits.

Another way to make large holes is to drill a line of small holes close together and join them up by cutting out with a hacksaw or a padsaw. You can use this method if you do not have a hole saw or if you want to cut an irregular shape and do not have a jig saw or a jig-saw attachment.

Deep holes can be drilled with shell or parrot-nosed augers; usually these are used in conjunction with a lathe.

Other bits are countersunk or counterbore bits, drill countersinkers (screw sinks), shaped to drill and countersink a hole for a given size of screw.

A plug-cutter is often used with a screw sink to conceal the screw heads in timber. The screw sink counterbores a screw to recess the head. A plug, cut from a piece of matching timber with the plug-cutter, can then be glued over the hole, and planed flat, becoming almost indistinguishable from the surrounding area.

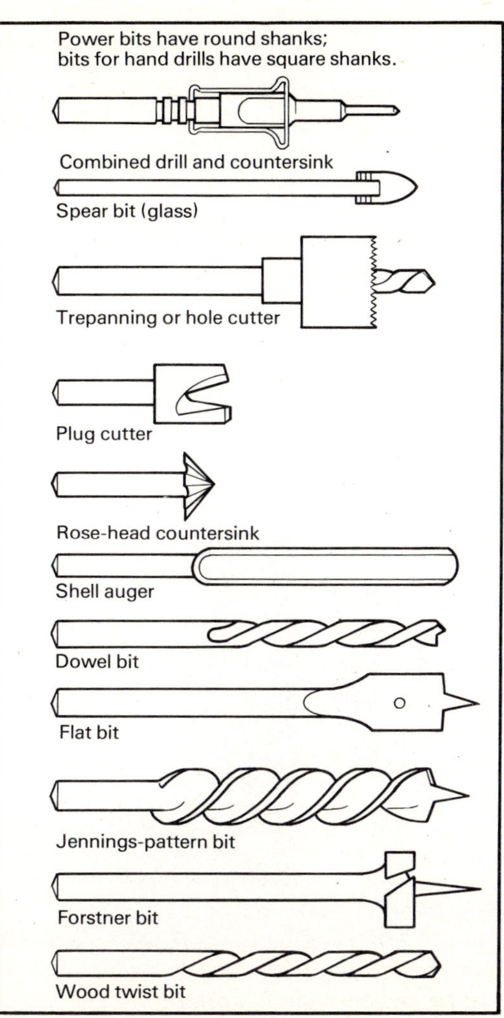


Masonry bits — the usual sizes are Numbers 8, 10 and 12 — are used to drill tough surfaces such as brick. These bits have tipped heads of hard material, such as durium or tungsten carbide, brazed into the tip.

When using a rotary percussion drill you should use a special bit, for the vibratory action may dislodge welded tips.

Some drill bits — both masonry and ordinary twist bits — have a thick piece of plastic fitted round the shank of the drill; this provides a depth indication, and you can move this up and down to establish the depth of the hole.

You can also make a depth stop or gauge by fixing a piece of adhesive tape round the bit — coloured tape is preferable as it shows up — and drill to the lower edge of the tape.

Various manufacturers operate a drill-sharpening service, which may include an initial free sharpening.

# The art of drilling

Different materials need different drilling techniques. For all materials, a variable-speed drill has advantages in that you can build up the speed you want, once you have made an initial impression in the correct place.

Ensure that the drill is unplugged before making an adjustment. Never make any adjustment at all with the drill plugged in — it is too easy to press the trigger accidentally and cause a nasty injury.

When inserting the bit, make sure it is inserted fully into the chuck and then tighten firmly with the key. Finally, check that the chuck is firmly locked.

When drilling very thin materials, put a backing piece beneath the work to protect the under-surface. This will also stop the work from bulging, spinning round or breaking.

Mark the position of the drill hole accurately and indicate the centre by drawing a cross on the surface. Dot-punch to prevent the drill from moving away from the intended position.

## Timber

Timber is drilled at a high speed. Place a piece of protective material, such as scrap timber, on the bench beneath the work to protect it, particularly for very thin timber.

It will ensure a neater hole on the side on which the bit breaks through and will prevent snatching on break-through. Use a clamp to hold the work steady and stop it from spinning.

Mark the hole position, place the tip of the bit on the mark and press the point into the wood. Before starting to drill, allow the drill motor to build up to its full capacity, which takes only a moment, then apply even, downward pressure on the drill.

Even with a backing piece beneath the work, the hole may not be perfectly neat but may have ragged edges. To achieve a really neat hole, put the work in a vice. Stop drilling the moment the point of the bit emerges on the other side; turn the work round, insert the point of the bit in the hole from the back, and complete the drilling operation.

If you are drilling into end grain, clamp the work on the bench and drill horizontally.

Where two pieces of timber have to be screwed together, three drilling operations are involved: making a pilot hole for the screw thread, making a clearance hole for the unthreaded screw shank, and drilling a countersink for the screw head.

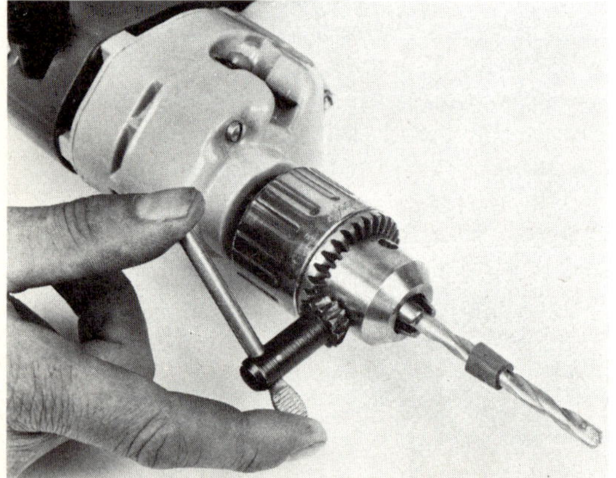

*Locate a bit squarely in the chuck, then tighten securely with the key*

*A try-square can be used beside the drill to ensure hole is square*

Combination drill bits are made for drilling three holes in one operation and usually possess an adjustable depth stop which regulates the extent by which the screw head is set beneath the surface. Combination bits are related to screw sizes.

## Masonry

Masonry is drilled at a slow speed. Mark the position for the hole, then put the tip of the bit on the spot and apply pressure; rotate the drill to one side and then the other, about the axis of the bit, without switching on the drill. This will make a slight groove, so that you have a purchase point and the motor is less likely to slip when you press the trigger.

Apply a firm, constant pressure. Withdraw the drill periodically, leaving it running, to remove debris and to stop dust from clogging the bit, as this may cause the motor to slow and stress.

## Concrete

The slow speed is used here, also. Concrete can be difficult to drill, for while the bit will penetrate the mortar elements, it is less happy when confronted with flint aggregates in the mixture. The bit may be deflected or stop drilling, and the tip quickly becomes blunted.

The rotary percussive (hammer) attachment is able to impact and break up the particles of hard material, but if you do not have a hammer device on your drill, or if you meet a really difficult obstruction while using a basic drill fitting, withdraw the drill and use a hand-held, hole-boring chisel and hammer to disintegrate the obstruction, then resume power drilling.

## Ceramic tiles

The technique used to drill tiles is similar to that used for drilling masonry. Use the same type of tipped bit, at a low speed. Again, place the drill bit in position and rotate the drill chuck about its axis to break the glaze. Use a firm pressure when drilling.

*Use a slow speed to drill masonry*

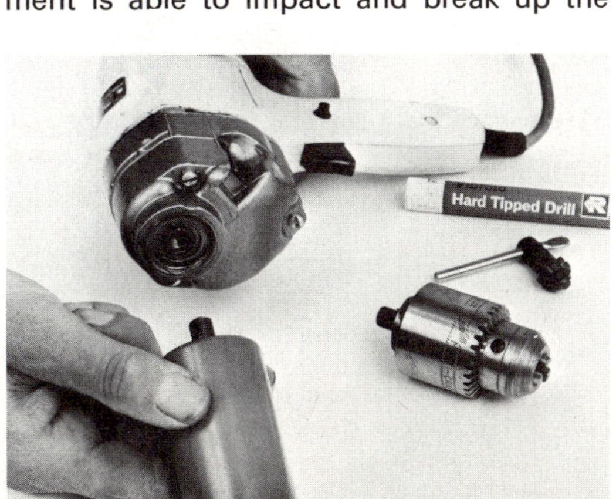


*Hammer attachment fits in drill shaft*

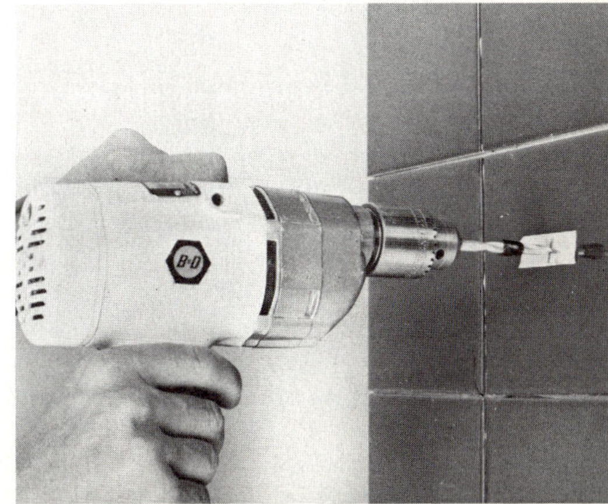

*Tape stops slip on smooth surfaces*

To stop the drill point from slipping on glazed or smooth surfaces, either tap the surface gently with a centre punch, so that the glaze is just marked, or fix a piece of sticky tape on the surface, to provide a purchase point, and mark the central drilling position on this.

## Glass

To drill glass, you need a spear bit, which is a small drill piece with a spear-shaped head. A masonry bit may shatter glass and is not recommended. Drill at a speed of about 350 rpm if possible — otherwise use the slowest drill speed you have.

It is advisable to wear protective goggles and to protect the hands when drilling glass.

Place the glass on a firm backing piece and lay it on a bench or any absolutely flat surface. Nail lengths of battening to form a frame round the glass to stop it from moving during drilling.

To establish the correct position for the hole, cross-measure from the outside edges of the glass to the corners. It is important when fixing mirrors that the holes are equally positioned. Do not drill closer than 13mm to the edge of the glass, or it may break. If possible, keep the drill at least 25mm from the edge.

From putty or modelling clay, form a small well around the drill hole position. Fill this with turpentine, white spirit or paraffin when drilling glass. (Use water for mirrors; oils would cause staining beneath the silvering of mirrors.)

When drilling a mirror, start on the non-reflective side; this prevents damage to the silvering. Avoid excessive down-pressure as this may fracture the glass.

Press the drill bit on the surface, rotating the chuck about its axis, to mark the surface and prevent the bit from wandering.

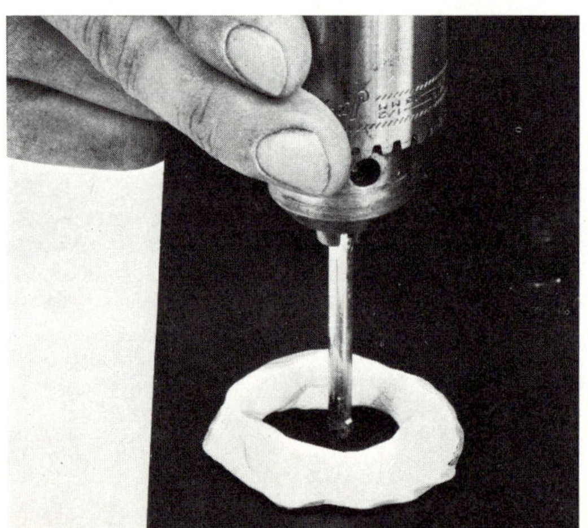

*When drilling glass, start drill by hand rotation inside lubricant well*

Then, with the drill running at its slowest speed, press gently on to the surface of the glass. Lift the bit from the hole from time to time as this helps the lubricant to circulate.

When you start drilling, rotate the whole unit slightly, while keeping the drill running to make sure that the lubricant reaches the bit point and keeps it cool. The spirit will turn white with powdered glass. When this happens, just add more liquid.

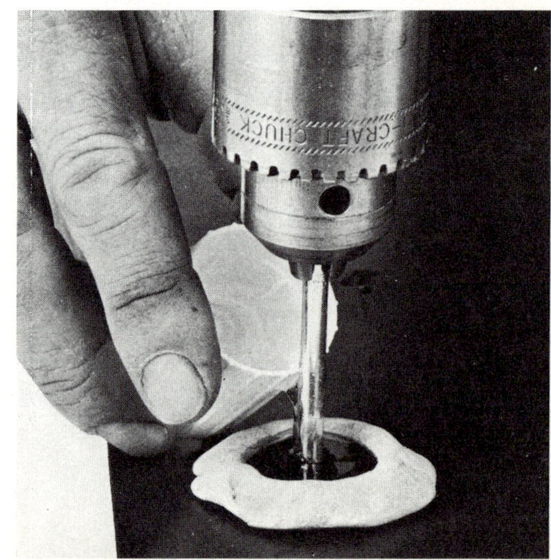

*Use slowest speed; stop drilling at intervals to add fresh lubricant*

You will hear a slight change of note as the bit starts to break through. Stop drilling, clear away debris, then drill from the other side. There is a danger that the bit may 'break out' a sliver from the face side of a mirror if you drill from one side only.

Once the tip breaks through, drill centrally from the other side and dab the drill tip with a soft brush dipped in lubricant. Take the 'wire' edge from the edges of the hole by rubbing it with a small piece of fine emery cloth wrapped round a pencil and moistened with lubricant.

If there is a slight chipping of the surface around the hole, do not be disappointed — this can be easily covered up by a dome-headed fixing screw and will never show.

When drilling in rounded surfaces, such as making a flex hole in a bottle for a table lamp base, you will not be able to form a pool of lubricant inside a mound of putty or modelling clay because of the rounded surface.

Instead, enlist help to squirt water on to the surface. A simple squirter can be made from an empty plastic container of washing-up liquid. Take great care, however, that you do not splash the drill and short-circuit the motor.

You can also keep the point moistened with a piece of absorbent cloth soaked in lubricant (to cool the drill tip), or a soft brush dipped in water.

The bottle should be well supported when drilling. You can make up a stout, improvised box so that the bottle rests firmly in this to help ensure that the drill bit does not slip, for this could cause the bottle to break.

An alternative method is to fill the bottle with sand to help break-through. The body of sand inside the bottle evens up the 'point' pressure of the drill bit and minimizes the possibility of cracking or breakage.

**Plastic laminates**
The laminate material should be rigidly clamped to a backing sheet at the point of drill entry. Use an ordinary wood twist drill, at a slow speed, to avoid heating up the plastic. To stop the point of the bit from skidding across the surface, place sticky tape over the spot, mark the centre with a cross, then drill.

For a hole larger than 6mm, work in two stages. You may chip the edges of the hole, so first drill a pilot hole, tape over this, then drill the main hole. Take care when the bit breaks through to the under-surface, as the tendency to 'snatch' is

greater on plastic laminate than on other materials.

**Metal**
Use a medium speed. When drilling metals other than brass or cast iron, which should be drilled dry, lubricate the drill bit with a thin oil for steel, or turpentine for aluminium.

Use high-speed steel bits. The pilot hole should be just big enough to take the 'web' so that it cuts at once and does not 'chatter' in the hole.

When drilling a hole bigger than 6mm, first tap out a centre mark with a centre punch, lubricate the area, then drill a pilot hole. Clamp thin metal to a piece of timber backing to reduce distortion and avoid jamming as the drill breaks through.

The hole saw is designed to retain the cut out piece on the centre bit or mandrel so that it does not fall to the bottom of the unit that you are cutting. Again, use fine oil or a metal-cutting solution to lubricate the cutting action.

First, punch a centre point with a centre punch and locate the mandrel point in this. The length of the mandrel bit should be adjusted to break through the sheet just as the serrated edge on the saw circumference starts to cut.

# Safety first!

*Whenever you make adjustments to a power tool, always unplug from mains*

A power tool is a strong friend — but misused it can be a deadly enemy! Treated with care and respect, it is perfectly safe, but there are a few sensible rules that you should unfailingly follow.

Regard power tools seriously, but do not be afraid of them; and certainly do not be deterred by the following rules of safety, which are intended not to alarm, but merely to warn of the possibilities of hazard, so that you can use the tools safely and with complete assurance.

The first rule is always to unplug any power tool from the mains when making any adjustments to it at all. Serious injury could result if the motor is started inadvertently when adjustments are being made — particularly if the hand is near the blade of a power saw.

Never use power tools in the rain or in the open under very damp conditions, and never leave them unattended when connected to the power supply — particularly if they are within the reach of children. Keep pets out of the way when using power tools.

Perhaps less hazardous, but still capable of causing serious injury, is the blade of a jig saw or a drill in the chuck bit — so always keep hands away from the 'business end'!

Remember, a power tool is used basically to cut, drill and abrade. It is driven by a powerful motor and is capable of doing a great deal of harm.

Even when the motor is switched off, the spindle of the tool will continue to spin for a few seconds. Allow the rotation to stop after unplugging the tool before touching the drill bit, blade or cutter.

To avoid the danger of the motor of a tool starting when it is not under proper control, make sure that the switch lock is disengaged before connecting to the power supply position.

All work pieces should be firmly clamped, or these may 'snatch' or spin, causing damage or injury.

A blunt drill bit may cause the drill to jam in a hole — and the entire body to spin round out of your hands. Keep drill bits sharp and holes free from debris.

A power saw can cut timber and many other materials effortlessly. Used correctly, it is perfectly safe. The saw is fitted with a safety guard that shields the blade. Many guards are spring-loaded, and snap back to cover the blade when the saw is disengaged from the work.

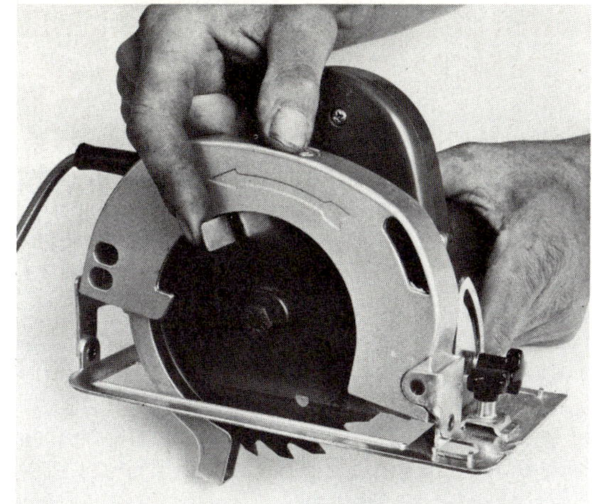

*Periodically unplug a power saw and check spring return action of guard*

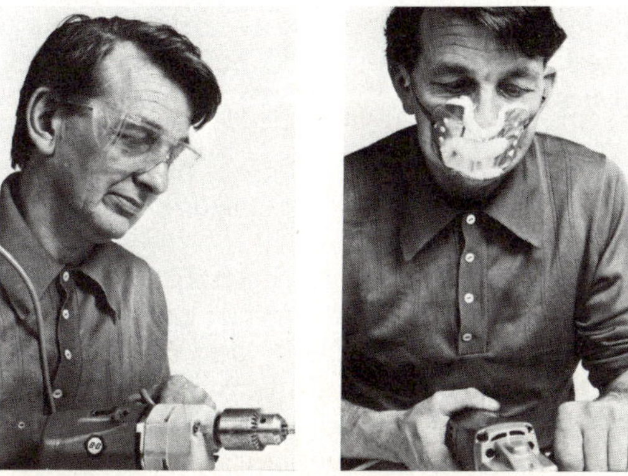

*Abrasive dust can be harmful, so wear safety spectacles or face mask*

The action of the saw when cutting pushes the guard back to expose the blade. Never operate the saw without the guard or with a defective guard.

After each cutting operation, unplug the saw, allow the blade to stop — remember, it will run for a few seconds — and then test the spring action of the guard.

When using a saw to cut abrasive material such as steel, always wear protective spectacles. These should be of a shatterproof pattern; a plastic pair with side-pieces is a sensible provision. The same rule applies when using a wire brush, as this also throws off fine particles.

Fine dust, particularly from a fine metal such as aluminium, or abrasive dust, can be a hazard to health. When working in dusty conditions, wear a protective face mask. This has replaceable gauzes which you should discard after about fifteen minutes of use.

A circular saw can be used with a saw bench. The saw fixes beneath the bench, with the blade upwards but with the guard in place, covering the blade until it is pushed back in operation.

Timber or other material should be held firmly at the outer edges when using the bench, with the hands well clear of the blade. For the last 50mm or so, use a 'push stick' to direct the material through. This consists of a piece of 25mm × 50mm scrap timber, with a notch at the end to engage the material.

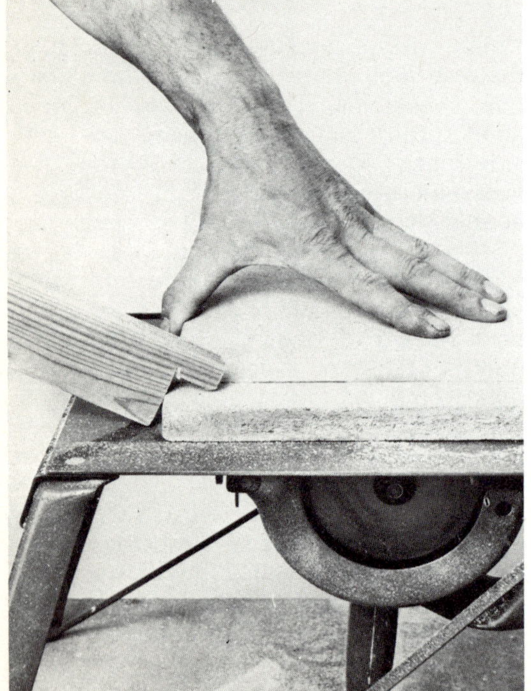

*Guide wood on bench with a push-stick*

Cables of power tools are not supplied with power plugs. It is best to use rubber-covered plugs and connectors with all power tools.

The cable contains wires that are coloured for easy recognition, and these colours, or an initial ('L' – Live, 'N' – neutral, 'E' – earth), will be marked at the connection points on good-quality plugs. Attach the wires to their respective points in the plug. Twist all strands tightly, so that there are no loose wires which could cause a short-circuit, and tighten and clamp the cable firmly in the plug. Discard any plug that gets broken or damaged.

Take care of the cable. Avoid walking on it or dragging it over rough surfaces. Keep it clear of oil and grease – and never use it to lift the machine or to pull the plug out of a socket.

Always keep cable well clear of your work area when the machine is stored.

The cable of a drill may easily be caught up in the revolving chuck or pulled round by the saw blade. Clamp the cable firmly in the hand and never allow it to snake or trail forward. Further, hold the cable under the arm, clamped against the body, or over the shoulder out of harm's way.

Care with clothing is also important. Never operate a power tool with loose, flapping clothing that may get caught up in the power tool. Ties should be tucked firmly in or, better, removed.

Sleeves should be buttoned or rolled up. Long hair is another possible source of hazard. This should be brushed well back – it is advisable to wear a hair net, to be completely on the safe side, if your hair is very long.

Rings and watches can also be sources of hazard – if, despite every care and precaution, the tool should slip in operation, it may catch on these and could cause serious injury.

A final important aid to the safe use of tools is a firm stance. Have both feet firmly on the ground and the legs slightly apart. Do not stand off-balance, and never work above your head or in any position where you do not have a firm hold on the appliance. Always concentrate on the work and not on the tool.

# Drill stands

There are two types of drill stand: the vertical and the horizontal. With the vertical stand and a power drill you can carry out accurate drilling at a true 90° angle, as well as face-plate tool sharpening.

The horizontal drill stand, with the power drill, is used mainly for driving rotary sanders, abrasive discs, polishing buffs and bonnets, grinding wheels and wire brushes. By adding a sanding table to the horizontal stand, you can shape, sand and grind objects.

The vertical drill stand consists of a base unit with slots for bolts to clamp the base to the bench or baseboard, a collar and a clamping bolt for the upright pillar, the pillar and the drill carriage.

You can raise or lower the drill carriage on the pillar by a locking knob, and you can adjust for depth of hole and the travel of the drill on the pillar by adjusting the height of the collar that clamps round the pillar. A return spring returns the carriage to the raised position.

You need only one hand to operate the handle and you can devise various jigs to tackle repetition work. You can also fit a drill stand vice.

When using the drill, clamp the cable out

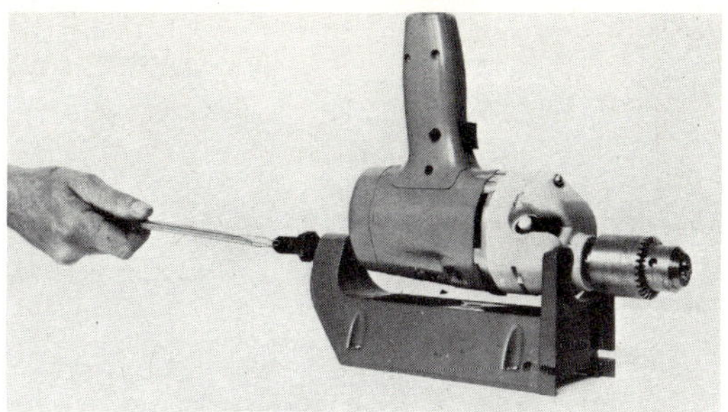

*Drill locks into horizontal stand*

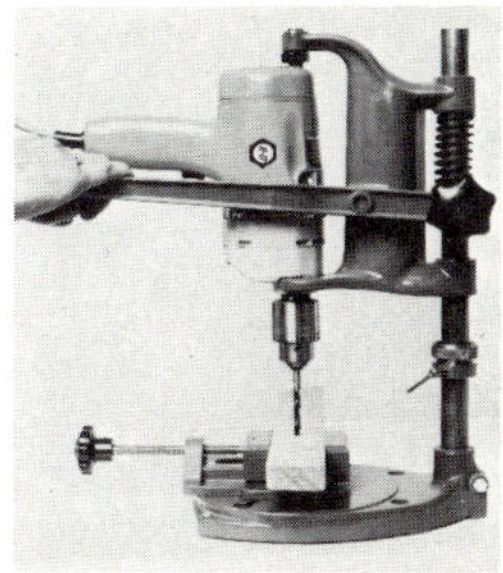

*Similar fixing is used in vertical stand*

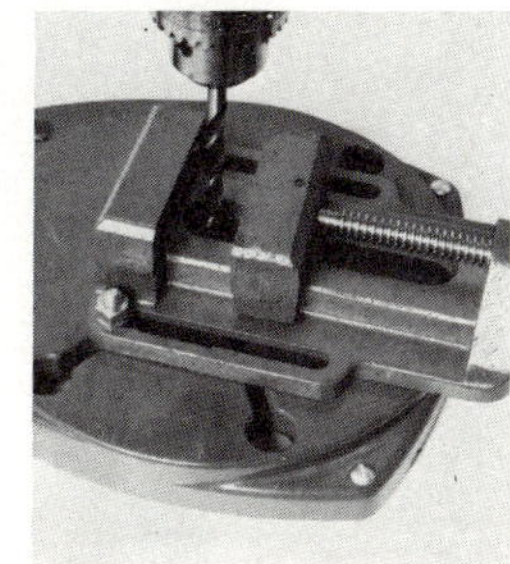

*Drill stand vice helps ensure precision*

of harm's way by winding it round the clamping handle of the cradle of the drill.

To keep the unit free from rust, wipe a film of light oil over the bright metal of the pillar. This will also enable the carriage to slide freely. There are slots in the stand base to allow you to drop through the head of a clamping bolt.

## Drill stand vices

This unit enables you to do steady work on the base of the stand. It is assembled in the following way.

Insert the coach bolt through vice slot from the under-side; fit the washer and engage nut on the bolt some one and a half to two turns, repeating for the opposite vice slot.

Drop the right-hand coach bolt head into the back right-hand keyhole slot on the drill base, and slide the vice and bolt to the innermost end of the base slot.

Tilt the vice to the right and engage the left-hand bolt head into the back left-hand keyhole slot and tighten the nuts.

When removing the vice from the stand, do not remove the nuts completely — always keep one or two threads engaged.

Clamp the work to be drilled in the vice, then move the vice so that the centre line of the hole to be drilled is exactly beneath the centre point of the drill bit.

Align, then tighten the vice, securing bolts and nuts fully with a small spanner so that it is firmly and rigidly clamped to the drill stand base.

# Right-angle speed changer

A right-angle speed changer enables you to drill at angles or in awkward spots. It may also be used with any drill fitted with a chuck, modified by using special adaptors; and, dependent on the way round it is fitted into the spindle of the drill, it either halves or doubles the speed of the drill.

You can also fit a grinding attachment. Do not use grinding wheels at a high speed unless you are satisfied that they are suitable: the maximum operating speed is marked on all good-quality grinding wheels.

## Uses

The speed changer enables the drill to work at an angle of 90° to the drive line. This enables you to drill, sand, polish or wire brush in awkward or otherwise inaccessible places.

The letters 'S', for slow, and 'F', for fast, are stamped on the flat face of the hexagonal drive adaptors at each end of the attachment.

When the drill is connected to 'S' and the chuck fitted to 'F', the chuck rotates at double the rated speed of the drill. With the drill connected to 'F' and the chuck fitted to 'S', the chuck speed is halved.

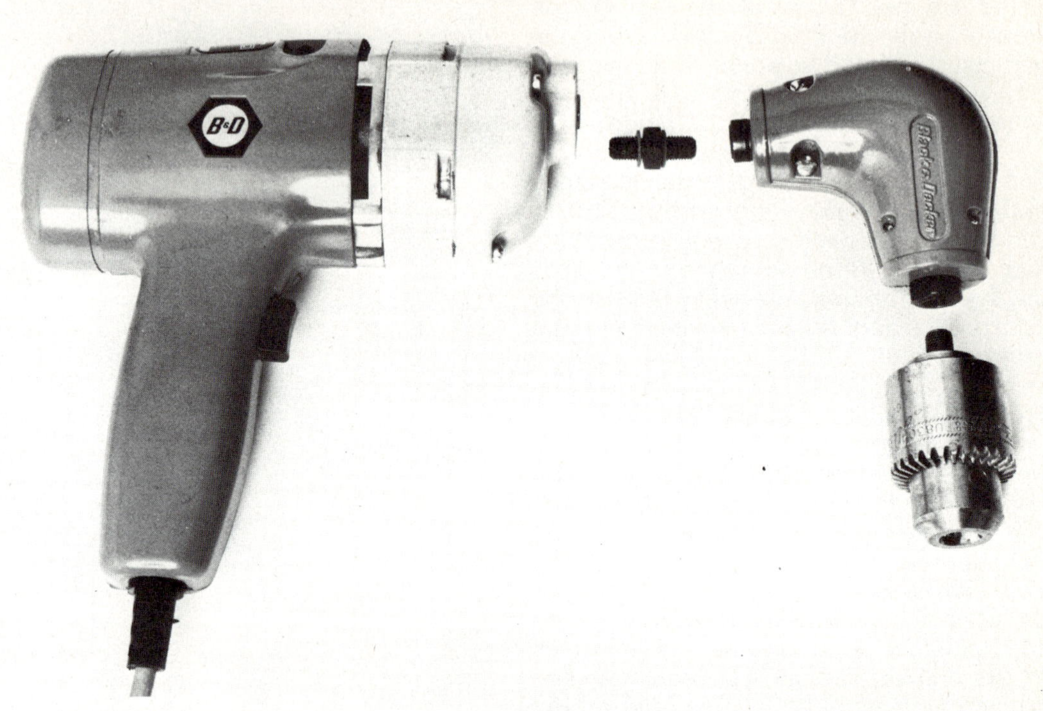

*Right-angled speed changer fits into drill's drive shaft and chuck goes on end. Unit can be used either way round, providing a two-speed choice*

Fast speeds are ideal for small-hole drilling and high-speed sanding; a lower speed is useful for drilling in ceramics, masonry, glass tile and brick, as well as for drilling larger holes in wood and metals, and for polishing.

## Assembling the speed changer

Remove the drill chuck by placing the chuck key into one of the holes, holding the drill in the left hand with the back of the machine towards you. Strike the key a sharp downward blow with a mallet or a light hammer, then unscrew it by hand.

Screw the stud adaptor into the drill in place of the chuck and tighten with an open-ended spanner. Ensure that the two fibre washers are in position, one on either end of the stud adaptor.

Screw the unit on to the stud adaptor, choosing the appropriate end of the attachment in order to obtain the speed required for the job in hand.

Screw the chuck or the accessory you are using into the other end of the speed changer and tighten the assembly with the spanner.

To remove the attachment after use, take off the chuck, fitting the open-ended spanner with the flats of the hexagonal adaptor by the drill spindle, using the spanner as the lever instead of the chuck key.

The unit can be fitted to any make of pistol-grip drill. You need a special chuck adaptor and a ball for other than Black & Decker drills. These are standard parts.

An additional chuck must now be fitted to the other end of the attachment. This can be an 8mm, 10mm or 13mm chuck.

**Operation**
The attachment gear is free to swing through 360° and will operate in any position equally well, merely by rotating it by hand.

When drilling small holes of 3mm or less in wood or metal, the high-speed connection has advantages. Penetration rate is increased and, because of the speed of rotation, small-diameter drills are less inclined to bend or snap. Disc sanding is best carried out at the higher speed.

The slow speed is best for use on masonry or for drilling large holes, screwdriving, polishing or with hole saws.

Hole saws cut most efficiently when the peripheral speed of the blade is correct. A speed of 1300 rpm permits the use of a 38mm hole saw, while at 2600 rpm the largest hole saw that could be effectively used is only of 16mm diameter.

The rounded shape of the attachment also allows access to drilling thick wood members such as floor joists where the overall length of the drill bit needed to penetrate the material, together with the

length of the attachment, may cause difficulties.

Place the tip of the drill bit a little above the point to be drilled and align the bit as near to perpendicular to the work surface as space permits.

Connect, switch on, and start to drill at the oblique angle, gradually bringing the bit nearer to perpendicular as it moves further into the wood.

Once the point is reached where the attachment enters the work space, bring the bit to a completely perpendicular position and complete the hole.

To remove the drill bit and attachment, reverse the procedure, but be careful to keep the drill running at its highest possible speed throughout the operation.

An alternative way is to start the hole with a much shorter drill bit, then remove this and substitute a longer drill bit. Push the long drill bit into the hole as far as it will go by hand and couple it to the attachment, then complete the drilling. Once again, the operation is reversed when extracting the drill bit.

# Polishing bonnet

*Lambswool polishing bonnet fits over the flexible rubber backing pad*

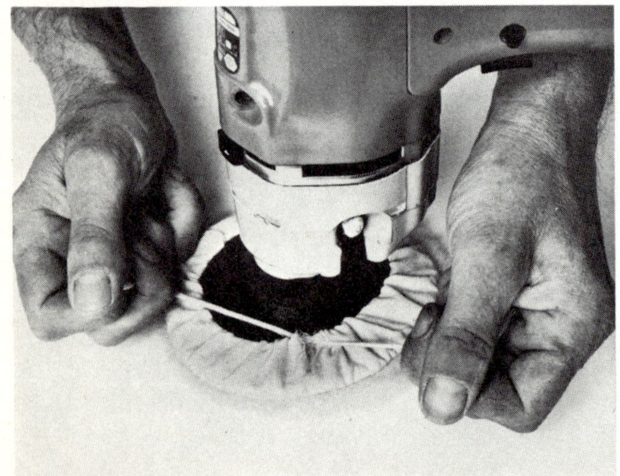

*The bonnet is secured on the pad by tightening up the drawstring*

The polishing bonnet is made of lambswool. It fits over the flexible backing pad and is tied with drawstrings.

When fixing the bonnet, make sure that it is centrally on the pad; otherwise it may not run true and could throw undue strain on the motor.

The bonnet may be used with the drill held freehand and can buff up wood, metal, plastics or glass — with or without polish.

Work up and down in even rows, applying light pressure so that the speed of the disc does the work.

Car polishing is one main application for the bonnet. First, wash the car with detergent or a car shampoo; for older bodywork remove discoloured film with a mild cutting paste. You can also use it to clean the car windows and chromework.

Wax polish the car, using long overlapping sweeps with the bodywork absolutely dry. Work in sections and in such a way that you do not trail cable over a part that is waxed or polished. Use the polisher set at a low speed, pressing lightly, with broad, straight strokes. Hold at an angle similar to that used with the disc sander (page 26), ensuring that only half the bonnet is in contact with the surface at any time.

You can use a buffing or polishing mop — which is not the same as the lambswool bonnet — with a drill in a bench stand to clean up brassware, cutlery, silver, pewter and many other items in the home that need polishing. Set the drill to fast.

If you want to polish a very small item, fasten it to a piece of wood so that you can hold it easily to the mop.

First, apply polishing compound to the mop by switching on the drill and holding the stick of compound lightly to the mop. Small pieces of excess fibre may fly off, particularly with a new mop, but this is nothing to worry about.

Get just the right amount of compound on the mop. If the mop gets wet without actually polishing, apply more polish. But take care — if there is too much polish you will get greasy streaks over the piece being polished.

You can scrape off excess with a semi-sharp object such as an old tobacco tin lid.

# Wire brushes

Wire brushes have 'bristles' made of hard, steel wires and are excellent for removing rust, corrosion and paint from a variety of metal surfaces, such as steel window frames or cast iron rainwater goods, before rust treatment and repainting.

Blemished brickwork can also be cleaned down before applying a sealant coat or colour-restorative treatment. You can also remove rust from garden tools.

A brush is more efficient than an abrasive disc fitted to a moulded rubber pad, as the wires are able to dig into the surface. However, take care if you are brushing a heavily rusted area that the wires do not tear through the metal.

Wire brushes may be either cup or wheel types. Wheel brushes are usually fitted on an arbor and into a drill mounted in a horizontal stand. The cup brush either fits in the drill chuck or screws into the drill drive spindle. Wire brushes should run at between 2000 and 3000 rpm.

When working with the drill freehand it is best to use the cup-type brush. Always wear protective goggles when working with a wire brush or wire wheel drill attachment.

*Polishing and abrasive set. Wire wheel, rag buff and abrasive disc fit to drill with arbor set. The polishing compound is used with rag buff*

*Wire cup screws into drill shaft*

## Wire cup brushes

Set the drill speed to fast. Place the brush on the work and move it away from you at an angle, in wide sweeps. The action is similar to that used with a disc sander. Once you have reached to the edge of the work, lift the brush clear, replace it on the work and move it forward again.

If you try to pull the cup back across the work the bristles will tend to become flattened. Use the wire brush so that the bristles are bent inwards rather than outwards.

If the wires become blunt they can be resharpened. For sharpening use a grinding wheel, a piece of sandstone or an ordinary brick. When using a brick it should be placed in a vice and the brush pushed across the surface at an angle of about 15°. Only one part of the brush should be in contact with the surface of the brick.

This type of brush is easier to use where the drill has to be taken to the work.

## Wire wheel brushes

The wire wheel brush is used with the drill fixed into a horizontal bench stand. This rigidity gives greater accuracy in work. While the wheel brush is best mounted in the drill chuck, it may also be used as a portable unit.

The correct stance when de-rusting a piece of metal on a bench is to have the wheel turning towards you. The worn strands then bite into the rust as they *meet* the surface and not as they leave it.

Hold the piece of metal on the underside of the brush. If it is placed on the top, the power of the motor tends to force the metal out of your hands.

## Wheel arbors

The wheel arbor can be used to mount a grinding wheel, polishing buff and a wire wheel brush. It is held between two washers and locked tight by an end nut, which has a left-handed thread so that it does not unscrew during rotation.

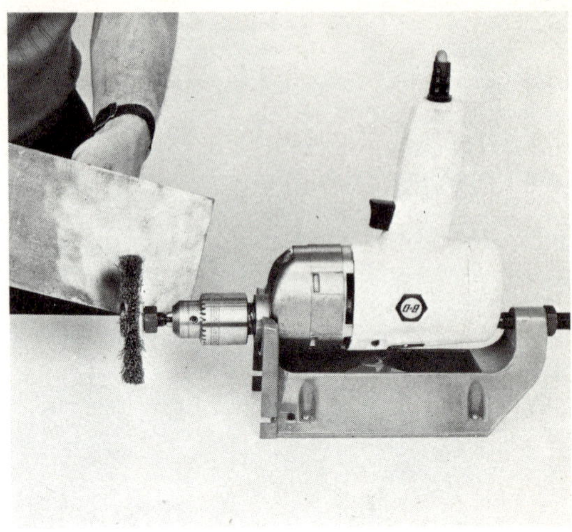

*Wire cup brush used to clean down rusty pipework; wear safety spectacles*

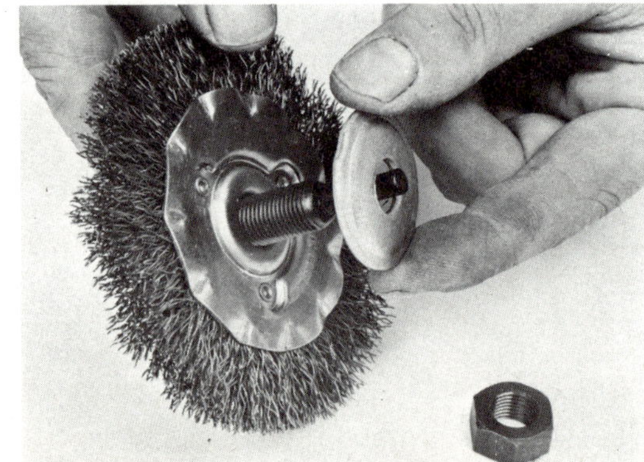

*Wire wheel brush fits to an arbor which then fits into the drill*

# Sanders

## Abrasive papers

Four grades of abrasive papers are more commonly used for all types of power sanding – fine, medium, coarse and extra-coarse. For general use, the first two grades are sufficient. Abrasive paper is made in sizes to fit the varying types of sander.

The finish on sanding paper depends on the number of particles or granules. Always store abrasive paper in a dry place. Fine paper is 150 grit; medium, 100; coarse, 60 and extra-coarse, 36 grit. Papers may be coated with grains of aluminium oxide, a man-made abrasive, harder than any natural abrasive, which is suitable for sanding wood or metal.

The grains are fairly widely spaced to allow the dust to fall away when the sander is lifted away from the surface to prevent clogging. The backing coat is tough and specially prepared to withstand the harsher action of the power tool.

Sandpaper and the term 'sanding' are generic terms. Sand is no longer used as an abrasive medium to produce an abrasive paper, and has long been superseded by more effective abrasives to give an abrasive surface. These include glass, garnet, emery, tungsten carbide, silicon carbide and flint. Glasspaper is the most commonly used.

Ordinary glasspaper is not suitable for power sanding as the bonding agent used is not strong enough to stand up to the harsh treatment of the sanding action. Close-grained glasspaper will soon clog and stop cutting. Never buy cheap sanding discs as they usually disintegrate very quickly.

These sanding papers can all be used with hand-held blocks, as well as in disc and orbital power sanders.

**Glass or garnet:** glass or garnet paper is used for a fine finish on bare wood; garnet is the harder-wearing paper.

**Silicon carbide:** this type of paper is known as 'wet-and-dry'. It is used wet to prepare painted wood or metal surfaces. As the silicon carbide material leaves a muddy deposit on the surface, this must be wiped off to prevent the paper from becoming clogged.

**Emery paper:** emery paper is used only to prepare metal surfaces.

**Tungsten carbide:** discs or pads of tungsten carbide may be used with orbital or disc sanders. Their great advantage is that they do not clog and have a greatly extended life.

## Disc sander attachments

The disc sander attachment is the most widely used for rubbing down a wide variety of surfaces, including wood, plastic and glass-fibre. It consists of a 125mm rubber backing disc which either fits into the chuck of the drill or screws into the drill spindle once you have removed the chuck.

*Flexible rubber backing pad screws into shaft in place of the chuck*

The screw-in version is better, for it is more positively housed. Also, because the disc is closer to the drill body, it is easier to handle. Again, having more than one disc fitted with paper to suit different jobs or jobs at different stages is a good, time-saving idea.

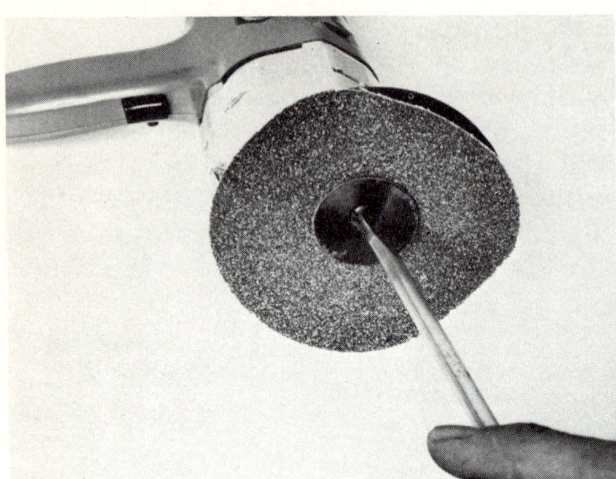

*Screw and centre plate hold the sanding disc in place on backing pad*

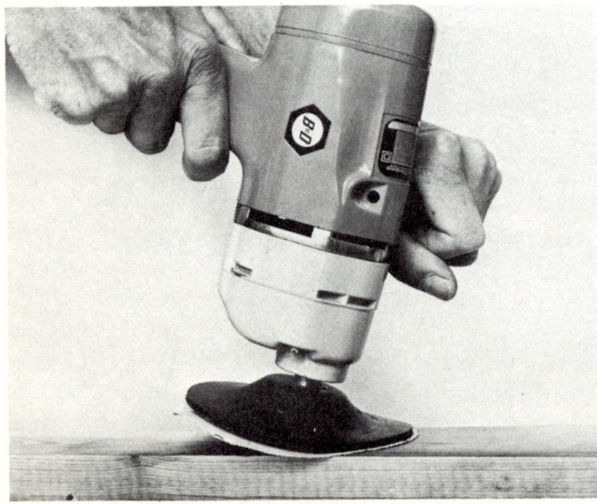

*To avoid swirl marks, maintain the backing pad at an angle when sanding*

The disc should be operated at a speed of between 1500 and 2500 rpm. The flexibility of the backing allows you to work round corners and do a great deal of shaping.

The abrasive discs fit to the pad by means of a centre locknut and plate. As the fixed disc rotary action may leave unsightly score marks on the wood surface, the disc should be used at an angle: work with the disc tilted at an angle of 30°.

Work with light sweeping strokes, as heavy pressure may overload the drill. Start with a coarse grit paper, working through to fine paper for the final finishing. If a very fine finish is required, it may even be worth while finally using a hand sander, or orbital sander with fine paper.

A disc sander is often used for removing old paint, but the friction set up between the paper and the paint surface may melt the paint, which is then driven into the surface and clogs the paper. Using tungsten carbide paper you avoid this problem to a large extent. Since bare wood should be sanded with the grain, do not use a disc for finishing but use a finishing sander.

There are various other types of specialized sanders.

## Drum sanders

Drum sanders are available in a wide range of widths and sizes. They can be used along the grain of the wood or across the grain. They can be used on flat, convex or concave surfaces.

A drum sander has a resilient foam cylinder mounted on an arbor. The arbor is gripped by the chuck of the power drill. A long strip of abrasive material is coiled up to make a band that fits round the cylinder.

*A foam-rubber sander which is designed to fit into the drill chuck*

The abrasive paper is held in place with adhesive. If the adhesive fails before the surface of the paper is worn, simply apply more adhesive to the non-abrasive surface.

As the cylinder spins, the abrasive edge is pressed against the surface being sanded. When the band becomes worn, you simply peel off the outer layer, and continue.

*Abrasive paper fixed round the drum produces a fine surface finish*

## Finishing sanders

An integral power finishing sander has the edge on a sander attachment in that it is always ready for use and does not have to be set up. In addition, the performance may be generally better.

The finishing sander is powered by a motor housed in a moulded case. It has a pistol-grip handle fitted with an on–off switch. A second handle can be screwed into either side of the case so that the sander can be controlled with both hands.

The trigger switch can be locked in the 'on' position. The trigger will then stay locked until you release it.

*Finishing sander with vibrating base plate produces a high-quality surface*

*Sander attachments*
The attachment is in two parts – the body, which holds the platen, and the eccentric drive adaptor, which couples the drill spindle to the platen to give the orbital action.

As the attachment is coupled to the chuck spindle the chuck must be unscrewed before the attachment is fitted. Screw the drive adaptor in the chuck recess in place of the chuck. Make sure that the fibre washer is in place on the spindle of the adaptor.

Unscrew the wing screw on the front of the attachment in an anti-clockwise direc-

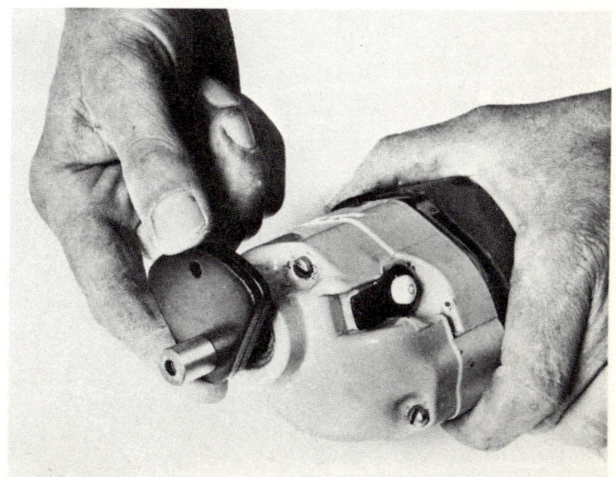
*Eccentric drive adaptor fits in drill shaft to couple sander attachment*

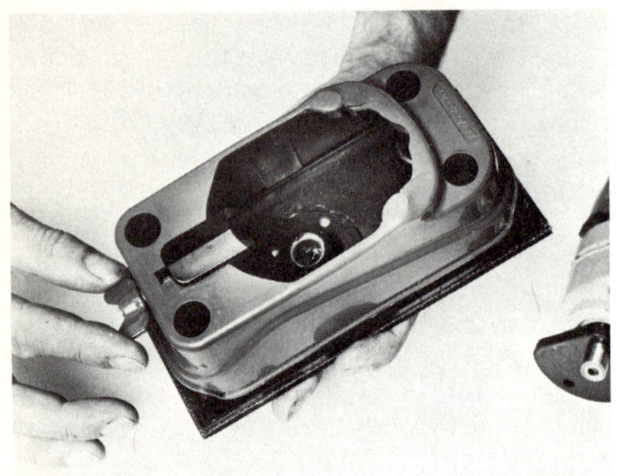

*The adaptor locates on to the base platten; first retract the wing nut*

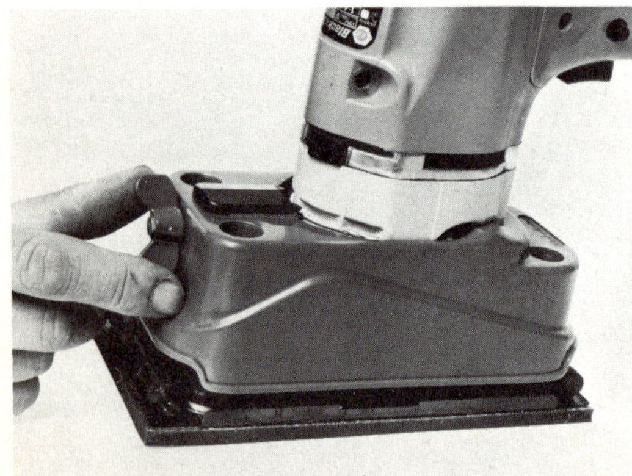

*Once attachment is assembled on to the drill, tighten up the wing nut*

tion as far as it will go, to retract the forked carriage. This allows the drill to be inserted through the top of the attachment.

Insert the drill into the attachment, tilting it slightly forward, so that the drive adaptor enters the bearing in the base of the attachment. Pull the drill back so that the attaching lugs locate in the recess in the rear of the drill.

When using single-speed drills, use the ventilation slots nearest the chuck to locate the lugs. The attachment is secured by turning the wing screw in a clockwise direction to secure the forked carriage in the front recesses of the drill.

Tighten the wing screw until the drill is held securely. Do not overtighten or you may damage the attachment. When you want to remove the attachment, reverse the assembly procedure.

Remove the drive adaptor, after giving the upper edge a slight tap with a light hammer.

*Sanding papers*
Fitting the abrasive paper and operating the sander are done in exactly the same way for both the integral tool and the attachment.

The base or platen of the sander consists of a sponge-rubber pad, and the abrasive sheet fits over this. The unit works with a high-speed orbital action in tiny circles, at about 4000 orbits a minute. This action, in all directions, removes surface high spots from every angle, so that you achieve a fine finish.

The platen of the sander, on which the abrasive paper is fixed, revolves in circles or orbits. For this reason it is sometimes called an orbital sander. When using an orbital sander, the whole of the abrasive paper comes into contact with the surface, the circular motion simulating the action of a sanding block. This type of sander can be difficult to use in recessed areas.

The abrasive sheet consists of strips of paper in various grades, 178mm long × 92mm wide. The sheet fits over the platen and is locked in at each end of a sprocketed wheel at the front and back of the platen or base.

The ends of the sprocket shafts are notched so that you can turn them with a screwdriver. Insert the paper in at one end, abrasive side up, ensuring that it lines up parallel with the platen, and turn the screwdriver in the slot to draw in the paper for about 25–50mm.

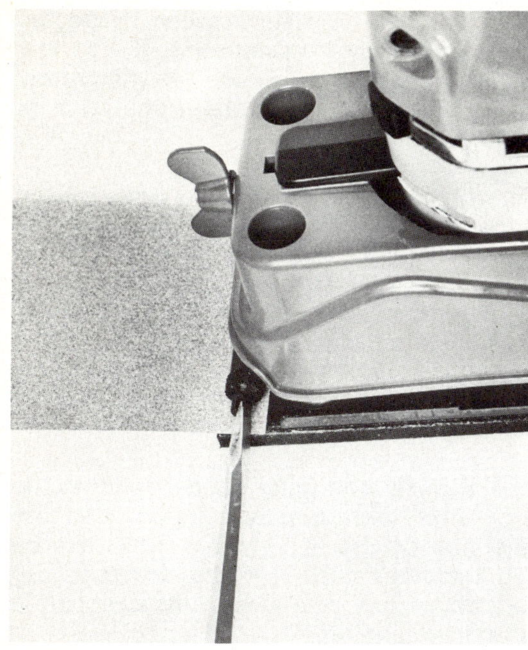

*Abrasive paper is fixed in place by turning notched screws on unit ends*

Similarly, slide the paper into the slot at the other end, and again turn with the screwdriver. Make sure that the sheet is stretched tight, or it may tear in use.

On some models the paper is held in by a spring plate. You gently prise this apart, at front and back, in order to insert the abrasive sheet.

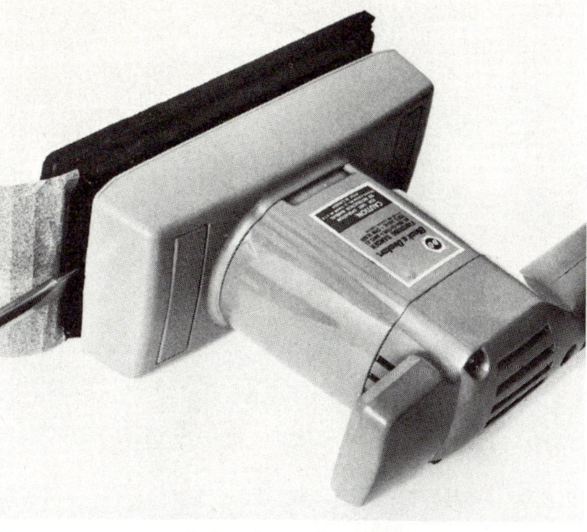

*On some models the abrasive paper is held in position by a spring plate*

Thick paper may tend to crack as you fold it. To overcome this, first rub the paper across the edge of the workbench. Draw the last 50mm over the edge of the bench to break up the adhesive in the backing. It is easier to insert the sheets into the paper grip if you first fold over two corners at one end. Fold them over tightly and then tuck them in at the other end. It also helps to trim the corners from the sheets where they fix beneath the platen.

### Using finishing sanders
The technique is the same for both the integral unit and the attachment.

Set the speed on a variable drill to the fastest setting. Switch on the motor, press the lock-on switch and start work. The action used is similar to that in planing.

Hold the drill in both hands, one on the trigger handle, ready to switch off quickly if necessary, and one on the side handle. Keep the cable out of the way. Move the unit backwards and forwards in straight lines, overlapping each row slightly.

You can work with or across the grain and can get a good finish either way. During sanding wood 'flour' will be formed which gets forced into the paper. Do not worry about this as it helps in the smoothing action.

*Finishing sander using side handle*

Remove worn paper immediately, otherwise the sanding action will press the platen too hard on the work; the platen will then act as a brake, slowing and placing stress on the motor. This reduces efficiency and forces you to press even harder, and may damage the drill.

The pressure of the sander's own weight will be sufficient on a horizontal surface. On a vertical surface, such as a wall, it is necessary only to apply sufficient pressure to keep the paper in contact with the work surface.

*Sander with a moulded hand support*

Odd patches on a surface can be treated in isolation by concentrating the sander action on the one place. Tilt the sander forward so that only the front edge is applied to the area.

The grade of paper used depends on the type of surface being treated and the finish required. Coarse papers are used to smooth rough surfaces down ready for final finishing with a finer paper. They will leave fine circular scratches, but these can be smoothed away with finer papers used in graduation until the surface is scratch-free.

If a surface is in fairly good condition, do not start with a coarse paper but use medium or fine. A very fine finish can be obtained by using a wet-and-dry technique on painted or varnished surfaces before the final sanding.

Before the final finishing, dampen the surface and allow to dry. This will raise the grain which can then be finally smoothed with the last sanding.

Always take great care when using electrical tools and water; use the water sparingly and work with an earthed or double-insulated tool.

*Finishing sander can be used to impart a bevel to a laminated surface*

It is a good idea to fix two sheets of paper at a time to an orbital sander so that the top sheet can be removed when it is exhausted and you can continue with the under-sheet. When preparing a large area, use two sheets of the same grade. For smaller areas, needing general and then fine finishing, fix a medium-grade paper on top with a finer grade beneath, changing to the finer grade when you feel the work is ready.

A finishing sander is an invaluable tool in decorating, for it can take the hard work out of the preparation of woodwork for painting. Stripped paintwork can be sanded down ready for painting and sanded again between paint coats.

This is useful for rubbing down the priming coat, which tends to bring up the grain of the wood. Do not sand too hard, however, or you may strip the newly applied primer.

A good stable base paint coat can be keyed with a sander. If you have a large area to prepare, it is better to use a metallic paper, which lasts longer when used for harsh work. A sander can also be used to rub down filled cracks or holes in wood or plaster.

*Sanding varnish surfaces*
A varnish finish will raise the grain of the wood. It is necessary to carry out all sanding before you apply the final finish, as after this it is impossible to sand again.

Sand until the surface seems satisfactory, and then dab white spirit over it to raise the grain. Re-sand and then apply the varnish finish: there should be no further risk of the grain's rising.

The 'give' in the platen makes it possible to work on curved surfaces. Flexibility can be increased by placing a piece of carpet or foam on the platen beneath the abrasive paper. The foam or carpet pad should be slightly longer than the platen to form a 'nose' covering the front.

When sanding round curves, only part of the abrasive pad may be in contact with the surface. This means that pressure is concentrated in a small area. Do not press too hard and keep an eye on the work or you may inadvertently remove more of the surface than you intend.

A piece of carpet also makes a good polishing or buffing pad if fitted in the sander in place of the abrasive and used face downwards. If the carpet is thick, part of the backing may have to be removed to allow the pad to fit under the clamps.

A metal or plastic surface can be made matt with a sander, ready for painting or a suitable finish treatment such as oiling. A sander can also be used to rub down a metal surface to provide a key for new paint, using a wet-and-dry abrasive paper.

While the bulk of the work of stone finishing is done with a sanding disc and a pumice stone, the finishing can be done with the sander. Lightly dampen the surface of the abrasive paper with water. As you work, a flour paste will build up, making the process a grinding-and-sanding operation.

You can also use the sander for chamfering off plastic laminate where it meets an edging strip. Fibreboard has a very rough edge, but with a finishing sander you can impart a first-class finished edge to it.

If you wish to shape polystyrene with a sander, just 'feather' it lightly, as this is a very fragile material. It is advisable to wear a face mask when doing this.

# Sanding and sharpening plates

**Disc-sanding tables**

The sanding and sharpening plate and the disc-sanding table fit on to a horizontal drill stand and are used with a power drill working at its fastest speed. The plate can also be used in a vertical drill stand.

**Setting up**

Remove the chuck from the drill spindle, screw the sanding and sharpening plate into the spindle, checking that it is firmly attached and the small fibre disc is fitted to the threaded spigot of the metal plate, as this makes it easier to remove the plate from the drill after use.

The drill must be correctly positioned in the horizontal stand. Hooked clamp bolts fit to both sides of the sanding table support to attach the sanding table to the yoke end of the horizontal stand or lathe headstock.

Pass the bolts through the slots in the outer edges of the stand frame to enter the square holes in the body of the stand.

Once the table is absolutely horizontal with the base, tighten the two clamp wing nuts.

Make the horizontal adjustment by slackening the wing nuts before tapping one or other side of the table top to adjust the setting.

Ensure that the table top is parallel with the sanding table by slackening the wing nut beneath the table top, then moving the table until its longer edge is the same distance at each end from the plate. After adjustment, make sure that you tighten all the wing nuts.

You can use the plate without the table in either the horizontal or the vertical stand. Principally, the drill fits into the horizontal stand (which is the same as the lathe

*Horizontal stand, sanding table and sharpening plate*

*Use a try-square to line up the table accurately*

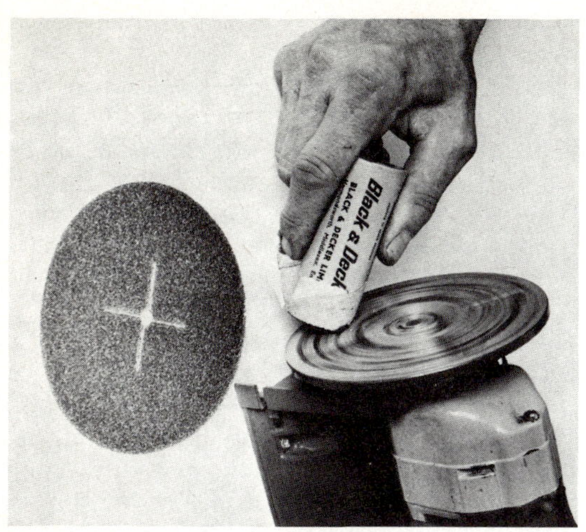

*Sanding discs are stuck on to sharpening plate with special adhesive*

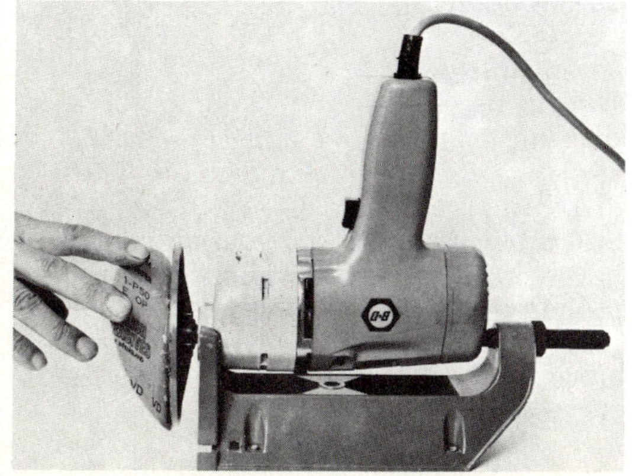

*The disc is pressed on to adhesive*

*Small items, such as scissors, can be sharpened using the face-plate*

headstock) for sanding, and in a bench vertical drill stand for sharpening. The horizontal stand is used the other way round as a lathe headstock.

When fitting the plate or the abrasive disc, always disconnect the drill from the power supply. Wear protective goggles when sharpening or grinding.

The disc table gives better control of sharpening, as the work can rest on the plate against the revolving plate.

You can sharpen general tools, workshop cutting tools such as chisels and centre punches, and household items such as scissors, knives and kitchen cutlery, using the plate.

Using the sanding disc with the sharpening plate produces less possibility of destroying the temper of metal than when using the grinding wheel, because the action is less harsh, with less build-up of heat.

The sanding discs, which are made in various grades for different types of work, are fixed on to the plate by disc cement, supplied in tubes.

To apply the adhesive to the plate, expose about 6mm of adhesive by peeling away the paper casing on the tube.

Operate the drill, and at the same time hold the disc cement against the revolving plate; this will spread a thin film of adhesive completely over the disc. Stop the drill and press the disc firmly and centrally on to the plate; ensure that it lies flat. You can then use the disc.

To operate, switch the drill to continuous running. The material you are sanding should be placed to the left of the revolving disc so that the disc will sand down into the work and it can be fed to the disc evenly.

Do not force the sanding action. Stop the abrasive paper from becoming overloaded with dust by keeping the disc moving alternately backwards and forwards across the disc, moving from the edge to centre.

To maintain a correct sharpening angle, when using the plate in either horizontal or vertical stand, slots can be cut in the sanding disc before fitting. These must correspond with slots in the sanding plate.

When you glue the disc to the plate, make sure that the slots are lined up. As the plate spins you can sight through the back of the disc and check the cutting angle. It is easier to use this method with the plate in the horizontal drill stand.

After sharpening a blade, give it a final honing on an oilstone.

## Using the stand without the table
You can sand timber, plastic, stone and ceramics using a sanding and sharpening plate, but the technique of sanding differs from that used when sanding with a flexible sander.

To chamfer material, hold it at an angle gently against the disc until the sanding action begins. Use the thumb and fore-finger as a guide to keep the work in position.

To clean up a rough sawn edge, hold the wood in the same way but not at an angle.

The tool can also be used to make a radius, leaving the sanded face smooth and exactly at right angles. You can also sand the mating surfaces of joints so that the finished job is square and at right angles.

## Changing sanding discs
Changing sanding discs is a simple opera-tion. Disconnect the drill from the mains and pull the worn abrasive disc away from the plate. Remove any old adhering cement by holding a blunt piece of metal

*With the sander plate and mitre guide, accurate angles can be formed*

or an old chisel against the right side of the plate as it revolves.

Apply new adhesive and press the new disc into place. If you are doing a lot of varied work, you can speed this up by using several plates, fitted with varying grades of abrasive paper, so that switch-over is speeded up.

## Removing the sanding plate
Rotate the plate until one of the metal ribs on the plate is just above the horizontal, viewed from the rear and from the right-hand side of the machine. Rest a small block of wood on the outer part of the rib and strike the other end of the block a sharp downward blow with a light hammer. This loosens the plate sufficiently for it to be unscrewed by hand.

## Mitre gauge
This is used with the sanding table, so that you can produce accurate mitres and angles. Calibration of the mitre gauge is in 15° intervals from 30° to 90°. Set this by loosening the wing nut and adjusting the pointer to the required angle on the pro-tractor scale. If you want an intermediate angle, set the pointer between the required calibrations.

The gauge slider runs in the outside groove of the table, the work being held firmly against one or the other side of the gauge leg. This is useful for making 45° mitre angles used in picture framing. It can also be used for sanding small items which might be damaged if hand-held.

The guide can also be used as an adjustable square. This enables you to mark the work out in pencil before cutting or sanding. Make curved or rounded ends by turning the work slowly through 180°, while holding it firmly against the revolving disc.

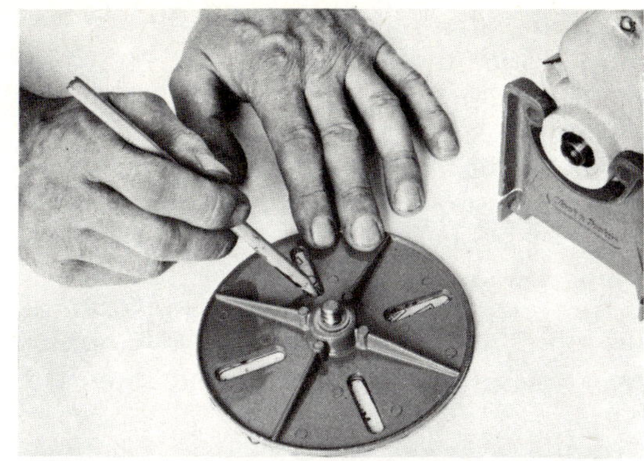

*'Sighting' holes can be marked on disc*

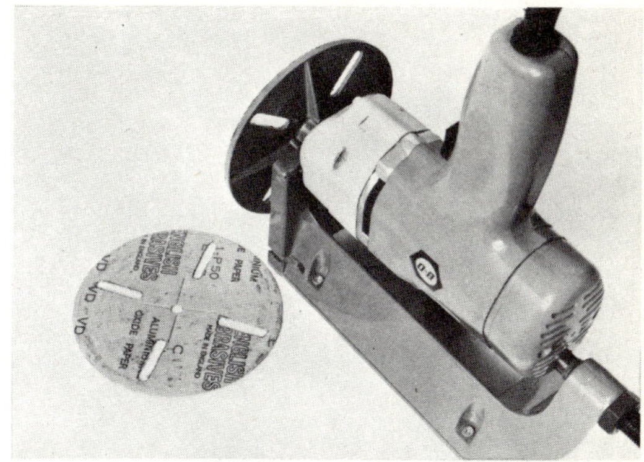

*Cut out and line up with plate slots*

*When replacing a worn sanding disc, first remove all old fixing cement*

*Angle of sharpening can be seen through back of the spinning face-plate*

# Drill-bit sharpener

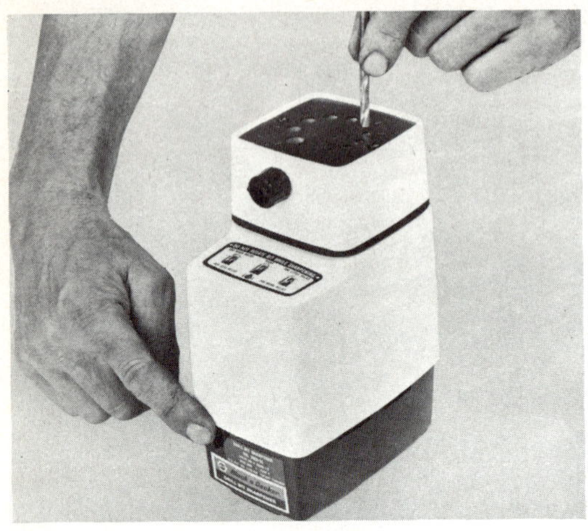

Sharp and accurate drill bits are essential when drilling. Drills blunt surprisingly quickly, but you can restore the edge on a grindstone — or you can use a drill-bit sharpener.

The drill-bit sharpener cannot be used for sharpening carbide-tipped masonry bits. Neither can you grind them on a stone — these bits have to be resharpened, where this service is offered, by the manufacturer.

There is an adjusting knob on the sharpener head to change the position of the bit inside the sharpener so that you can control the cutting of the first two angles.

Place the sharpener on a flat surface and plug it into the mains. Set the adjusting knob on the front in the vertical position, insert the bit in the smallest hole of the index or top plate into which it will fit. If you put it into a larger hole, it will result in a poorly shaped bit.

If the point of the bit is not in the centre, the bit will drill oversized holes which may not be located exactly where intended.

The bit will tend to 'walk', or drill holes that are not round. You can control the point position by the length of time that you switch on and by the pressure you apply on the bit when sharpening.

Turn the knob in a clockwise direction to increase the angle of cutting, and in a counter-clockwise direction to decrease the cutting relief.

For small bits, move the knob only slightly in either direction; for larger bits, move it a little more.

Drill bits must be sharpened dry — do not use water or any other coolant. Normal sharpening causes the bit to become hot, so do not put your finger on the tip immediately after sharpening it.

Push down and rotate the bit clockwise until it stops. Keep the hand in the same relative position for the entire sharpening operation. Do not rotate the bit when sharpening.

Hold it in the downward position, with a medium pressure, for between one to three seconds, then release. Do not remove the bit until the wheel has stopped turning, which takes two or three seconds.

Pushing down too hard on the bit can cause it to heat up excessively and result in its losing its temper or hardness.

Smaller bits take less time to sharpen than larger ones. Remove the bit from the sharpener and mark the side sharpened with chalk or a grease pencil (Chinagraph). Rotate the bit half a turn, or 180°, re-insert into the top plate opening and repeat the sharpening procedure.

Too little or too much cutting relief can be corrected by turning the front adjusting job clockwise, for more relief, and repeating the sharpening process.

Make only slight adjustments. The sharpening cycle may have to be repeated a number of times if the bit has been broken or badly worn.

# Power grinders

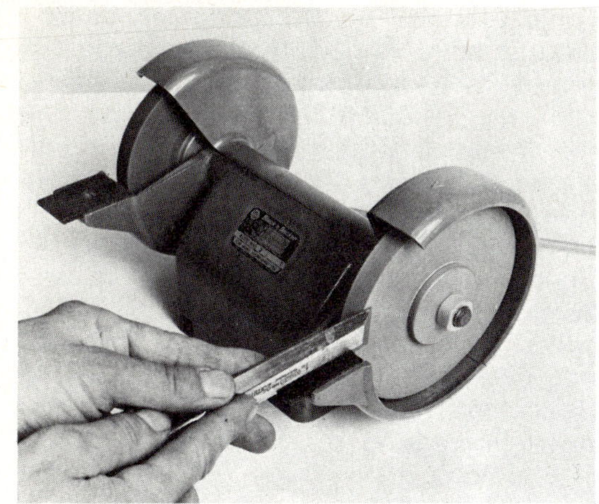

*Grinder, with coarse and fine wheels*

This takes over where sharpening and grinding on a face-plate leaves off. Bench grinders consist of two wheels, one coarse and the other fine, revolving at a speed of around 4000 rpm.

A rest on each wheel enables adjustment to be made to compensate for wheel wear.

By reversing the rest of the fixing screw, fine adjustments can be made on a slot in the clamping plate. The wheel is shielded around most of each edge for protection.

Four clamps enable the grinder to be fixed to the bench or clamped to a firm baseboard.

It is advisable to connect it to a switched power source and, of course, unfailingly to disconnect from the mains whenever you have to make any sort of adjustment to the unit.

Adjust the two tool rests so that they are just clear of the wheels, then lock the fixing screws. The angle adjustment is mainly for grinding and sharpening cutting tools. For most work, set the rests horizontally.

Ensure that the rests are not so far away from the wheel that the tool you are sharpening is able to be drawn into the gap, since this could result in hazard. The recommended gap is 3mm.

Among the jobs you can do using a bench grinder are trimming and smoothing metal — a job you otherwise do with a file — and sharpening hardened steel.

A grinding wheel is capable of producing a spectacular firework display. Do not be alarmed by the shower of sparks that will be produced when using the tool, but do always wear protective, shatterproof goggles.

## Grinder attachments
Where a power drill is used with a grinder attachment, multi-speed drills should be

set to work at the higher speed. Remove the chuck from the drill by placing the chuck key in one of the keyholes and giving the end of the shank a light tap with a hammer in the usual way.

Place the power drill in the horizontal stand of the grinder. Screw the locking bolt into the recess in the drive unit and tighten the nut lightly.

To mount the grinding wheel, screw the grinding wheel spindle into the threaded shaft. Mount the washers with the grooved sides towards the grinding wheel.

The safety guard is mounted over the grinding wheel. Two hook bolts with washers and nuts hook into the stand, so that the guard is firmly attached to the stand.

The eye shield can be adjusted to various angles with the wing nut. A slot in the eye shield holder allows the distance between wheel and shield to be varied.

The distance between the work rest and grinding wheel can be similarly adjusted to 3mm.

Before starting work, make sure that the power drill is firmly mounted into the horizontal stand and that the safety guard

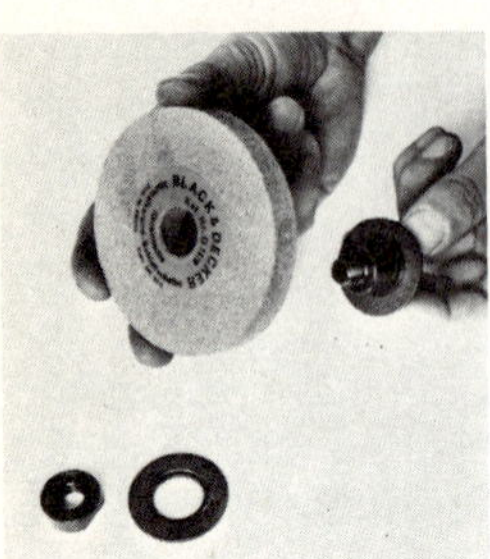

*Grinding wheel assembly for attachment to a drill*

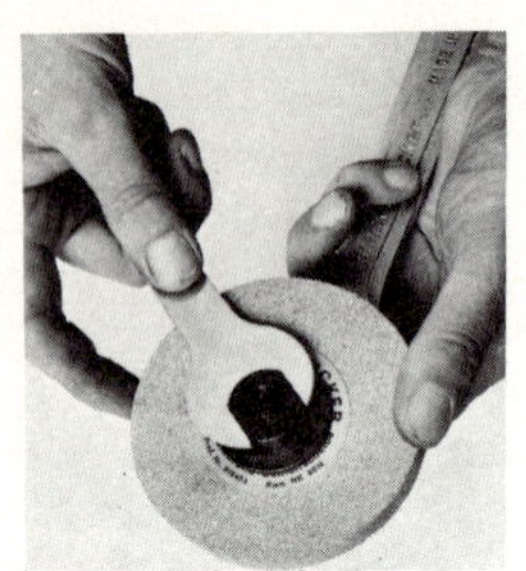

*Arbor assembly is tightened on to grinding wheel*

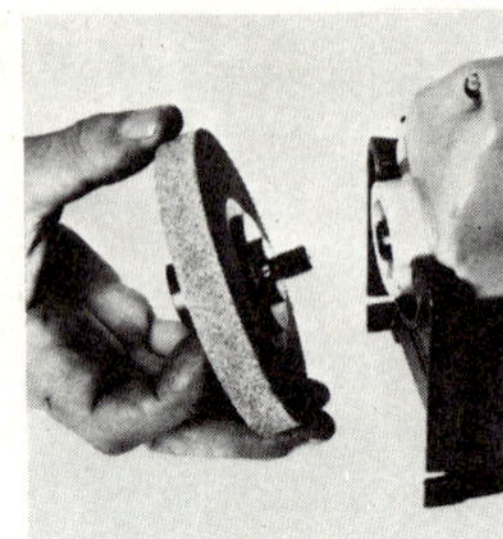

*Drill fits on horizontal stand, arbor in drive shaft*

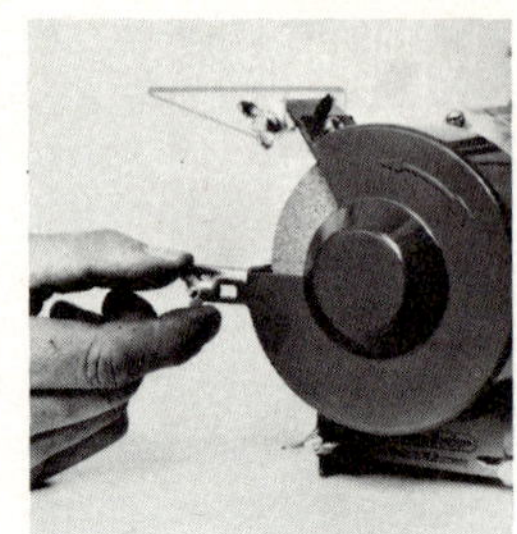

*Safety cover, shield and tool rest are then fitted*

is firmly attached to the stand with the hook bolts.

If you need to remove or replace the grinding wheel, remove the safety guard by loosening the hook bolts. Fit a spanner to the spindle nut and give the end of the shank a light tap with a hammer.

Remove the washer and the grinding wheel from the spindle, then fit the new wheel on the spindle.

To use, switch on, hold the tool flat against the rest and lightly against the wheel. Keep the tool moving across the face of the wheel and never press against one spot, for this results in uneven wear on the grinding surface.

Take great care not to wear away the squared wheel edges, or the wheel will become rounded and will then grind unevenly.

Do not normally use the wheel to grind soft metals such as aluminium, copper, brass or lead, or plastics, as this clogs up the wheel surface, and may mean that you will need to have the wheel professionally redressed unless you can skim the resulting encrustation off with a hacksaw blade.

Avoid overheating the tool when sharpening, especially when grinding hardened and tempered cutting tools. Tempered metal will turn blue and lose its cutting potential.

While grinding shapes the edge of a tool, you will need an oilstone to finish off and add the keenness to the cutting edge.

Tools used in woodworking are usually ground on one side. Rest the blade flat against the rest front but sloping upwards, with the bevelled edge resting on the wheel face. Maintain an accurate grinding angle and move the blade evenly from side to side.

Once you have ground the bevel square, the blade can be finished off by being honed to a sharp edge on an oilstone. Use a light oil, preferably *neatsfoot*, on the stone and lay the blade flat on the stone, increasing the angle by 5° to 10° as you hone it.

Maintain a figure-of-eight movement over the stone and inspect the edge from time to time. Finally, turn the blade over and remove the 'wire edge', which will be raised on the flat, by rubbing the blade flat against the stone.

## Grinding angles

| Tool | Grinding angle | Honing angle |
|---|---|---|
| Block plane | 30° | 25° |
| Plane irons | 25° | 30° |
| Paring chisel | 20°–25° | 30° |
| Chopping chisel | 30° | 35° |

Wood-turning chisels are ground on each face with identical bevels of around 45°. Gouges are ground on the outside angle to an angle of at least 45°.

# Angle grinders

*Both shield and rest are adjustable*

Knives can be ground by a continuous stroke along each side of the blade to produce a cutting edge of about 20°. This is easiest carried out on the side of the stone.

Scissors are sharpened by opening each blade and laying it flat on the rest parallel with the front face of the fine stone. Set the rest at an angle of 10°, which will give a cutting edge of 80°.

Draw the blade across the stone in a single movement to restore the sharp edge and take the wire edge from the back on an oilstone.

Do not grind the inside face of the blade, since this may be hollow ground and possess an accurate curve which is needed to cut properly.

Shears and hedge-clippers are ground in a similar way, and you should again avoid grinding the inside faces of these blades. Take care when grinding near the tip, since the reduced amount of metal can get very hot and 'draw' the temper of the steel.

Lay screwdrivers flat on the stone with the shank against the edge of the rest and the blade tip upwards. Cold chisels are ground and sharpened at an angle of about 40°.

The top of a cold chisel flattens out and cracks after a period of being hammered. Since small chips may fly off and could be hazardous, it is a good idea to grind the top of a flattened chisel with a slight inward taper.

Centre punches are ground by holding them to the wheel at an angle and slowly turning the shank to grind to a point of 60°.

To change grinding wheels, unscrew the spindle nut and take out the worn wheel and chucking plate, reversing the order to fit the new wheel. The left-hand spindle has a right-handed thread, and the other way round for a right-hand spindle. Make sure that you use a wheel suitable for the speed of the grinder.

Angle grinders are widely used in industry and are now coming into everyday use in the home. A compact and light-weight version of an industrial angle grinder, the Black & Decker Grindermite, is finding an application in domestic use.

This has a wide variety of applications including cutting metals, masonry, sharpening edges and sanding down and dressing surfaces. A face mask and goggles should be worn.

The term angle grinder relates to the plane of the wheel in relation to the drive shaft. The wheel is used at an angle. The cutting or abrading disc or wheel is on the same plane as the body of the machine; a straight grinder has the cutting surface on the end of the motor drive, at right angles to the body.

The Grindermite has a no-load speed of 9000 rpm and accepts grinding wheels and cutting discs of 115mm size. It can, using the correct grinding wheels or flat, reinforced cutting discs, cut metal, masonry or compositions such as glass-fibre.

Metal-cutting discs and wheels incorporate aluminium oxide, for use on ferrous metals, and silicon carbide, for use on non-ferrous metals, masonry and composition materials.

To fit the disc, mount the inner flange on the spindle and position the disc on the flange. Secure by placing the outer flange on top and tighten by holding the spindle with the spanner supplied and turning the outer flange clockwise with the pin key, also provided.

Always ensure that the maximum permissible speed marked on the disc is above the maximum rated speed of the machine.

When using the machine, apply only sufficient pressure to keep the wheel firmly in contact with the object you are cutting or grinding.

Excessive pressure will slow the machine and reduce the grinding performance, in addition to wearing the disc much more quickly.

The machine is supplied with a side handle, which can fit on either side, for either-handed operation. An on—off switch is mounted on the top of the machine towards the back. The shield is adjustable to give the maximum shielding from sparks

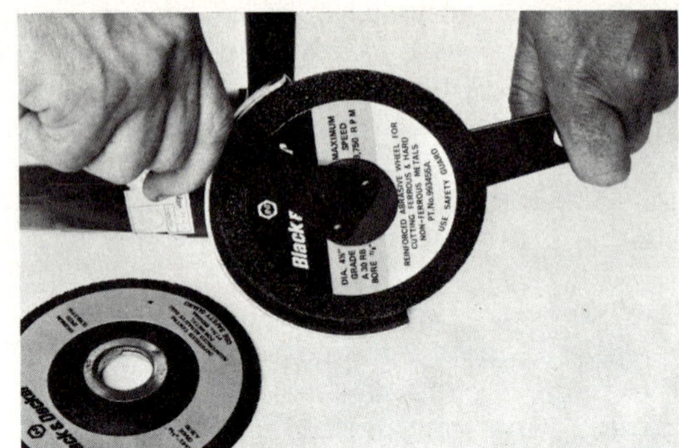

*Grindermite disc locks on with spanner*

*Discs are used to cut through materials*

for either-hand use.

Ensure that the adjustable guard is positioned to deflect sparks away from yourself when using the machine.

If the machine is accidentally stalled, switch off, wait a few seconds, switch on again, and the machine can be re-used.

With this high-performance machine it is important that the carbon brushes are checked every fifty working hours and replaced when they are reduced to one-third of their original length.

The grease of the gear case should also be changed once every 500 hours. Make sure that you do not overfill the gear case. Suitable grease can be obtained from one of the maker's service branches.

# Circular saws

*Versatile, industrial pattern saw*

The circular saw is a fast and accurate power tool. It can cut, quickly and without fatigue, a wide range of material with great accuracy.

Using the correct blade — or in some cases cutting discs — you can cut thin-gauge ferrous metals, aluminium, lead and soft metals, asbestos, marble, slate, ceramic and quarry tiles, bricks and mortar, abrasive timbers, such as laminated chipboard, and laminates — in addition to timber.

The saw can be either hand-held, or fixed in a saw bench, which further increases its versatility, particularly for carrying out fast, repetition cutting.

A saw can consist of an attachment to a power drill, or an integral unit. Whether used as a bench-mounted or hand-held unit, guide and mitre fences help to ensure accurate and clean cuts. An industrial pattern saw, though more expensive, is a wise buy and will give you greater power and greater scope than even the integral saw unit but cannot usually be bench-mounted.

An integral saw is more powerful than an attachment. An average saw blade turns at around 2000–3000 rpm.

## Saw blades

Saw blades have teeth similar to those of a hand saw but set around a circular steel blade. The blade cuts continuously so, unlike a handsaw, does not need to be pulled back at the end of a stroke. Therefore it cuts far more quickly.

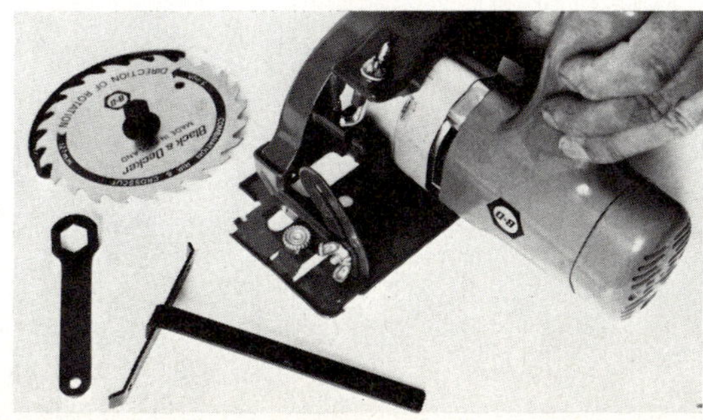


*Saw attachment clamps on to drill body*

The teeth are angled slightly outwards. This is called the 'set' and makes a slightly wider cut than the actual width of the blade. This helps to reduce friction between blade and the sides of the cut, and speeds up the operation of cutting. You should allow for the width of the cut in your measurements. The cut made by a saw is called a 'kerf' — the old English word for 'carve'.

Saw blades must be kept sharp and correctly set.

*The right saw blade*
Saw blades are classed according to the number of teeth or 'points' they have: the more points, the finer the saw cut. There are two main sizes of saw blade – 125mm and 150mm. (There are larger blades for the more versatile industrial saws.) The range of saw blades makes possible the cutting of wood, metal and plastics.

A 125mm blade gives a depth of cut of 40mm and the larger blade, 50mm. Blades are available in several sizes and patterns.

**Rip blade:** used for coarse cutting with the grain.

**Combination rip and cross-cut blade:** suitable for most purposes, such as cutting thick or thin hardwoods and softwoods, with or across the grain; also suitable for cutting softwoods, plywood, hardboard and blockboard. It usually has a standard 125mm 24-point blade. The blade has teeth that rip but also provide a reasonably clean-cut line across the grain of timber.

**Cross-cut blade**: for man-made boards or for cutting across the grain. A blade with a 6-point set is generally best.

**Planer blade**: this gives a superb planed finish. The blade is hollow ground, thinner at the centre than at the teeth. It has no sideways set and deep, widely spaced gullies, for clearing away waste. A variety of thick or thin materials can be tackled. These blades, in particular, should be kept sharp and run at maximum revolutions to avoid clogging, as this may cause the saw to bind and the motor to slow.

**Tungsten carbide-tipped blade**: used for hard or abrasive timbers, laminates, Contiboard and other chipboard products.

**Metal-cutting blade**: cuts aluminium, copper, lead and soft metals.

**Abrasive disc (silicon carbide)**: shatter-resistant, used for cutting marble, slate and ceramics.

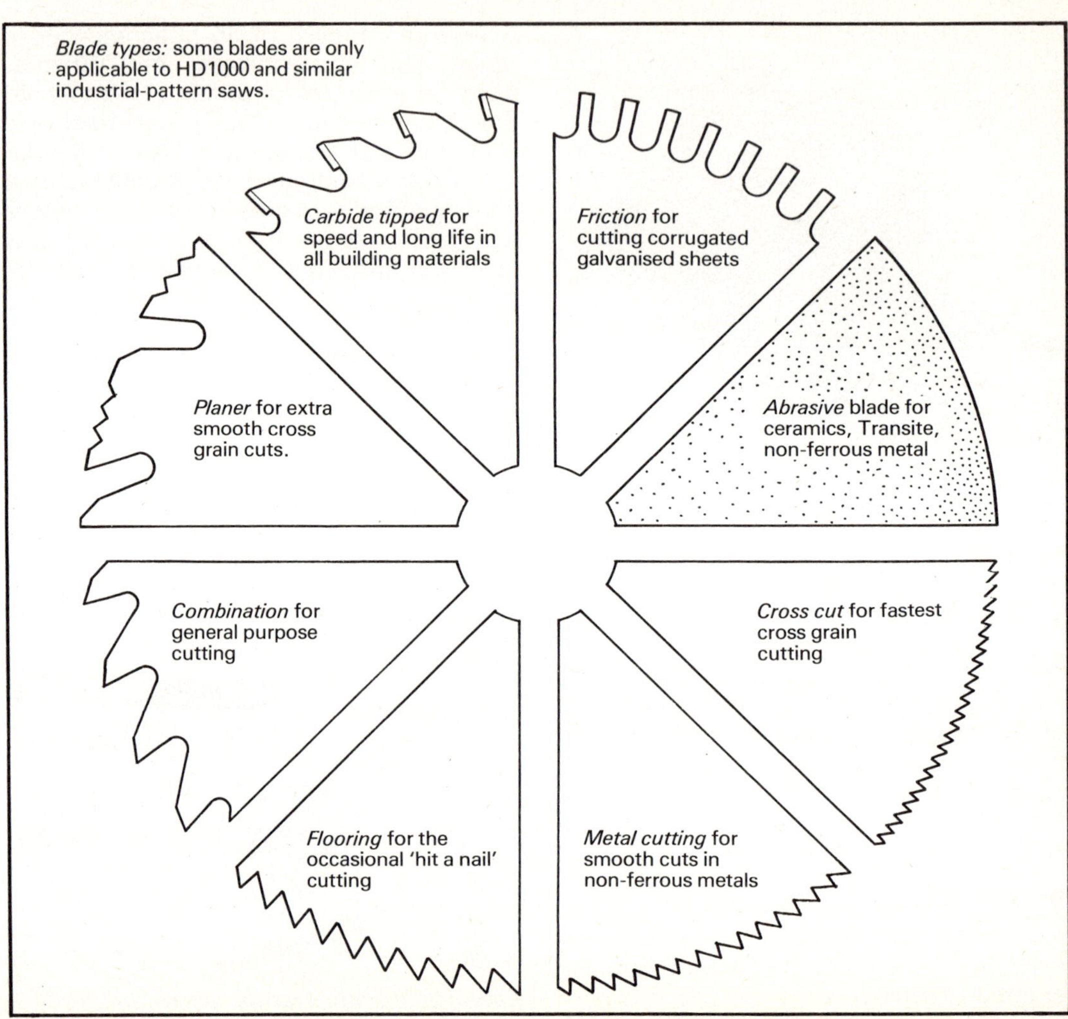

**Abrasive disc (aluminium oxide):** used for cutting thin-gauge ferrous metals such as drainpipes, gutters and steel cables.

*Fitting a blade*
The saw blade must be fitted so that the cutting edge strikes the work. The maker's name should face outwards and be visible through the blade guard.

*Changing a saw blade*
Saw blades usually have a hole in the blade, so that you can insert a screwdriver to stop the motor mechanism from turning when tightening the centre locking nut with a spanner.

Insert a screwdriver in the hole of the saw blade and housing, then loosen the blade-retaining bolt with a spanner and remove the blade.

Pull back the blade guard with the guard grip. Place the new saw blade, inscription uppermost, into the housing through the slot in the base plate. Check that the arrows on saw blade and housing point in the same direction.

The blade must be inside the black guard and centralized on the drive spindle. Place the washer on the blade-retaining bolt and screw on the blade. Align the holes in the saw blade and housing, then finally

tighten the retaining bolt.

Never attempt to fit a blade or make any adjustments with the unit plugged into a power point.

**Saw attachments**
A portable saw attachment consists of a main frame, handle, combination rip and cross-cut saw blade, guard, fence, securing bolt and washer.

This is designed to fit to the power tool with the chuck removed. There is a fixed upper blade guard and pivoted lower guard which pulls back in use and on some models is spring-loaded to return to cover the blade when released from the work. The shoe can be adjusted for depth and for sawing at an angle.

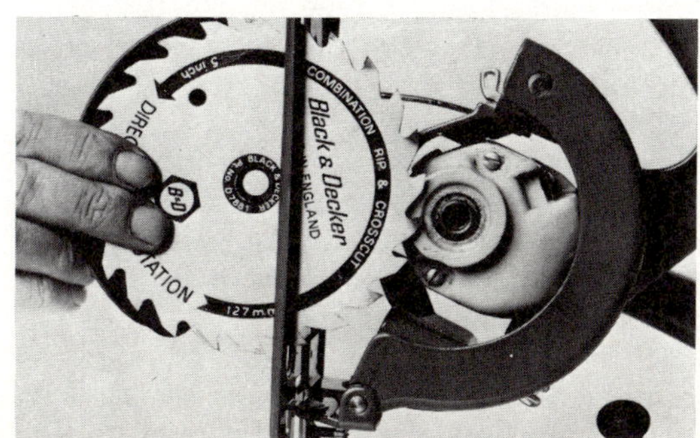

*Check that the saw blade goes on with the lettering on the outside*

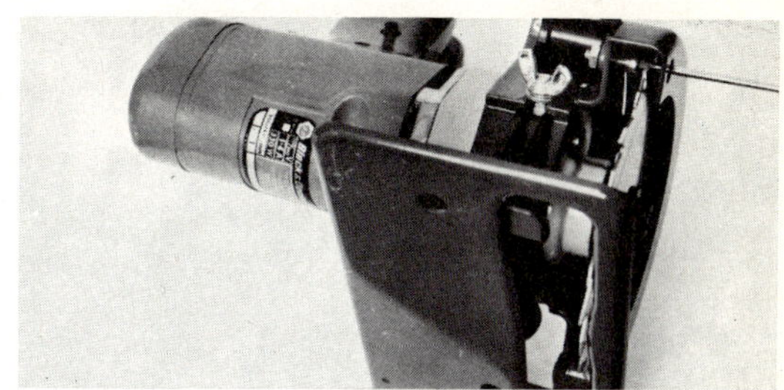
*Tighten the guard on saw attachment*

The unit fixes to the drill by a hinged clamp, with lugs that fit into the front slots on the drill case, and is held in place by a single wing nut. When using a saw attachment with other than a single-speed drill, set the drill to the highest speed before operating.

All saws and attachments have an adjusting screw to control the lowering of the shoe or base plate of the main frame. Normally, on domestic power saw blades, this is to a maximum of 30mm.

Before use, check that all the nuts on the saw are tight and guard action is correct, then plug the tool into the mains.

A drill trigger has a lock-on switch. When a saw is bench-mounted, or if you have to make long cuts, it is useful to have the saw running constantly — though take particular care.

*Give the lock nut a sharp tap with a soft hammer to release the nut*

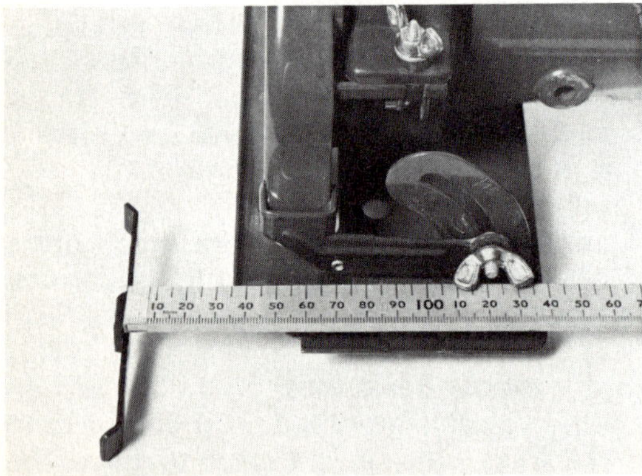

*When using the rip fence, the width of cut may be set by measurement*

*Set cut depth slightly deeper than material*

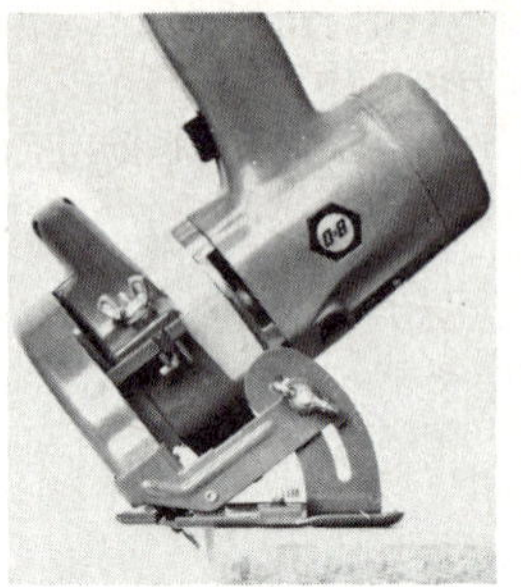

*Saw can be adjusted to cut at an angle*

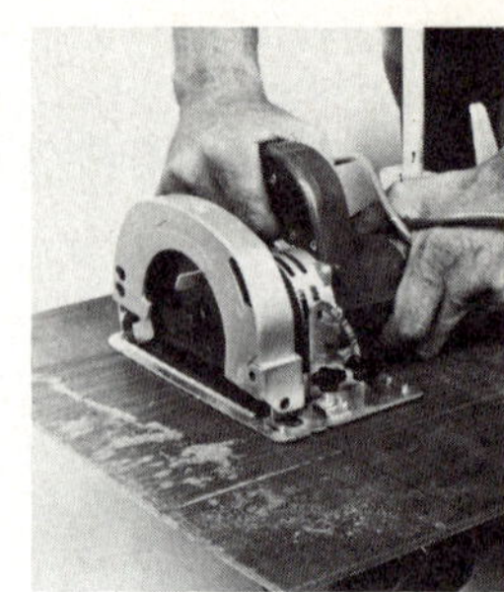

*Saw can be used freehand or with saw bench*

Before plugging in a saw, always press the trigger to release it in case it has been accidentally left locked on when previously used.

## Rip fence

The rip fence guide helps you to cut timber accurately, either across the grain (cross-cutting) or along the grain (rip-cutting).

The fence fits into a slot in the power saw or attachment; the width is adjusted by measuring with a rule. Measure from inside the stock to the outside of the teeth, pointing towards the drill.

Its angled T-section runs along the straight edge of the timber to keep the saw running on course. The fence can be fitted on either side of the power saw and gives a cutting width of about 165mm when fitted on the left-hand side, but only about 75mm when fitted on the right.

Any problem of width can usually be solved by turning the timber round and working from the other direction.

A rip fence is supplied for use with the saw table. A bench mitre guide allows you to saw the face of the timber at any angle; it slides from the front to the back of the table in a slot parallel with the blade. The front of the guide has a protractor which allows it to cut at an angle.

Improved control of the rip fence can be provided by extending it with a piece of battening screwed on the inside face of the fence, through two holes in the bar of the fence.

These are easily drilled out if there are no holes in the fence. Do not extend the fence beyond the centre of the saw blade, for the blade may jam if you run slightly off-line.

## Mitre guides

A mitre guide is also provided to enable you to cut across a board or other material at any angle. You can extend the guide by screwing a piece of battening to it through the pre-drilled holes in it.

Clamp the piece of material to the batten when sawing to ensure that the blade does not bind or run off.

A waste piece of plywood is a useful fence extension as it can protect delicate materials, such as veneers. You can, however, saw along a marked line without a rip fence with care.

## Depth of cut

The depth of cut can be varied so that you can cut completely or partially through a piece of material, such as timber. When cutting timber, set the blade so that it just protrudes through the work, as this allows the teeth to strike at a better angle. Correct adjustment also causes less working friction, cutting down the load on the motor.

Make the depth adjustment while holding

the saw against the work. Check carefully that the adjustment is correct. If you are in any doubt, make a sample cut on a scrap piece of similar wood.

## Sawing at an angle

Sawing at an angle to the vertical is achieved by adjusting the sole plate so that it is at an angle to the saw. A protractor scale, standard on most power saws and saw attachments, enables the shoe to be pivoted and set to a pre-determined angle, from a 5° to a 45° tilt in 5° steps, so that the saw will then cut at an angle when the sole is placed flat on the work.

## Adjustment to cutting angle

This angle is set by loosening the locking knob and adjusting the base plate until one saw blade tooth juts out below the material to be cut. Firmly tighten the knob. You must allow for a slightly deeper cut

*Angle cuts can be bench- or hand-held*

*When sawing on bench, push evenly from each side with hands well clear*

to compensate for the angle. Allow for this in setting the guide to line up with the cutting notch on the front of the saw. For example, when making a 45° cut, the saw should protrude through the sole of the attachment by the thickness of the work plus 6mm.

To cut grooves, set the saw depth slightly less than the depth of the required groove. Make two passes for the outer edges, followed by a series of intervening parallel cuts, leaving only a thin wall of wood between each. Do not cut away all the wood, or the blade may slip out of grooves. Finish off by removing the remaining pieces with a firmer chisel.

Before starting work, see that the work is clean and dry; brush dirt or grit from old timber. Check for nails or screws, metal fastenings and other obstructions that may damage the blade. Keep the cable out of the way of the work, and trail it back, well clear of the moving parts.

Grip the handle firmly when operating. Place the shoe of the saw on the work, switch on the motor and allow it to build up to full speed.

Once the motor has attained full revolutions, ease the blade gently into the work. Do not push the appliance too hard into the timber; keep it moving forward at a constant pace.

Move the blade steadily and do not rest in the cut or this may overheat the blade and blunt the teeth. Do not change direction, or you may jam the blade.

The motor should do the work — aim for an even motor hum; if the note falls sharply, the motor is under tension, so slow the pace.

Keep the shoe plate flat to the top of the material and gently move the saw forward. At the end, allow the motor to run for a few moments after cutting.

To prevent the saw cutting into and damaging the bench, position the work so that part of it slightly overhangs it. For example, when cutting a 75mm strip from a 225mm wide board, allow the 75mm to overhang the bench, so the bulk of the material on the bench supports the saw.

After use, wipe the blade clean and smear with thin oil to keep it bright.

Work involving the technique of ripping must be secured firmly so that your full attention can be concentrated on the job in hand.

When cutting a long length of timber, the cut section may tend to close behind the saw blade, causing it to bind. This can be remedied as follows. Once you are about a quarter of the way along the cut, stop the motor and insert a small wedge of wood, such as a matchstick, in the cut. Ease the saw blade back from the edge of the cut, restart the motor and complete sawing.

The material must be held against the thrust of the teeth for the blade to cut. The cutting action on a bench-mounted saw is from the teeth top downwards, supported by the bench. (With a hand-held portable saw, the saw works above the timber surface, with the teeth cutting from below and upwards. The wood is supported against the base plate, or shoe or sole of the saw.)

**Cutting large sheets**

When cutting large sheets of timber, such as blockboard, the width of the cut required is too great to use the rip fence. Sheets have to be supported equally when being cut. You can use four boxes of equal height to support the sheet at corners, or you can support it with four battens, two for each half of the sheet, placed on the floor, with the blockboard laid on top.

The battens should be thick enough to prevent the saw blade from touching the floor — and they should not impede the blade. Another way is to use a Workmate portable bench with extension arms.

Accurate straight cutting over a long length can be achieved by clamping a batten at each end along the cutting line and keeping the sole of the saw pressed against this while cutting, or by marking a pencil line against a batten or straight-edge fixed along the cut line.

Some attachments have two notches in front of the sole, which can be used as line-cutting guides. One notch is for vertical cutting; the other for cutting at an angle of 45°.

You can lightly clamp or nail a batten to the face side of the material and keep the

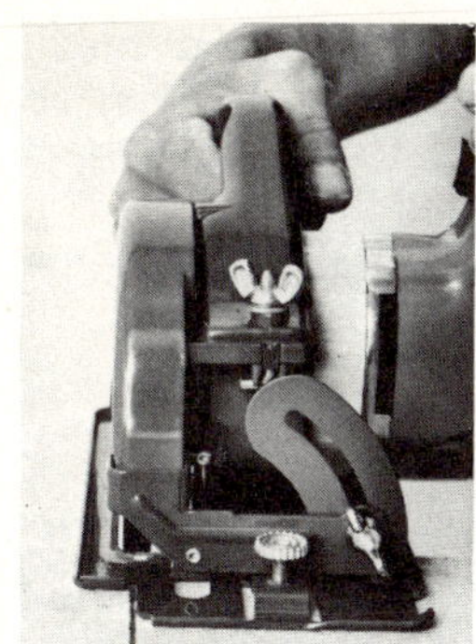
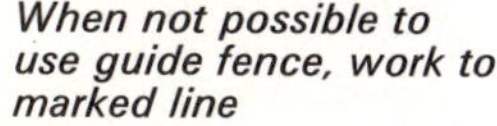

*When not possible to use guide fence, work to marked line*

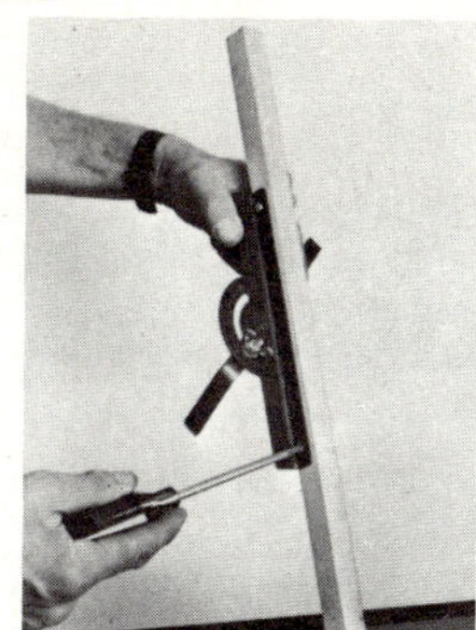

*The guide fence can be extended by screwing on a piece of timber*

edge of the shoe parallel with this. This is also useful when cutting a board at an angle.

## Pocket cutting
This is a technique for starting a cut in the face of a piece of material. This requires care as it can be dangerous. Avoid using a drill with an attachment, as this has not the power of an integral unit, and can catch and judder. Set the saw to just beyond the depth of the wood. Rest the back edge of the shoe on the surface and carefully turn the movable, lower guard back to its full, open position – up to its stop.

Release the guard and tilt the tool forward until the saw blade is just clear of the wood surface. Press the trigger and carefully lower the saw, maintaining pressure on the back edge of the shoe.

Allow the saw to cut into the surface before pushing it slowly forward. Release the trigger after cutting, allowing the blade to stop before lifting it from the cut.

## Bench sawing
A saw bench turns a portable power saw into an even more versatile tool, able to carry out a wide range of jobs in precision woodworking, as well as providing a means of effortlessly cutting and rip-sawing timber.

The saw bench consists of a flat table top on legs. The saw slots into and is held by spring clips. The guarded blade protrudes through a slot in the middle of the table.

You can adjust the height of the blade, and thus the depth of cut, by moving the saw up or down from beneath. The legs are detachable and simply bolt on to the bench table top. You can release the saw by inserting a screwdriver in the slot in the bench top and pushing down the clip.

Check that the saw blade is parallel with the slot in the saw table and adjust by edging a screwdriver between the side of the shoe and one of the fixed lugs. Make

*An extended rip fence provides greater control of the work on the bench*

sure that the spring-loaded clip is firmly engaged so that the saw cannot jump out. Lock the blade on when the saw is used on the bench.

Both saw fences can be taken off so that large sheets of material can be cut. In use, check the angle of the rip fence from time to time, as the blade may jam if it is not truly parallel with the fence. On some power saws, slip clutches disengage the motor if it comes under stress.

Timber, particularly, is likely to slip on a saw bench because the action of the blade tends to push it back if it is not firmly held. Timber needs to be held firmly.

The saw bench should be firmly fixed to a work bench or other firm surface. However, as with other power tools, this can monopolize bench work space and it is a good idea to make up a baseboard, cut from blockboard, which can be clamped into the bench vice; alternatively, the baseboard can be inserted into the jaws of a portable bench such as the Workmate.

Mount so that the saw is at right angles to the bench. If you cut a hole out of the centre of the blockboard it gives more working space to make adjustments beneath to the saw.

*Cutting a mitre using the mitre guide which fits on to the saw bench*

## Bench rip-sawing
Adjust the depth of the saw cut so that the blade protrudes slightly through the work; this puts less stress on the motor.

Next, position the rip fence. This slides into a base plate on the saw and is calibrated, usually in centimetres (1cm — 10mm). To cut a parallel line, for example, 10cm from the outside edge, align the figure 10 on the rip-fence graduation with the mark for a normal vertical cut and then tighten the knob to lock the fence.

Place a ruler on the bench, using the thumb and forefinger as a stock, and move the fence into position. Take the measurement from the inside edge of the fence to the outside edge of the saw teeth.

## Angle sawing
Many different angles can be cut on the saw bench. First, mark the angle on the end grain of the length of timber. Adjust the saw to the same angle and then rip-cut in the normal way along the length of the timber.

Mitred picture frames can be made by marking the frame sections at an angle of 45°. Position the saw vertically, then cut to the gauge.

While saw benches usually have metal fences, you can fix a strip of thin plywood to these to prevent metal-to-wood contact which could damage delicate surfaces; it also enables the length of the fences to be extended.

## Cutting with the grain
Switch on the motor, and allow it to pick up speed. Feed the work piece slowly and steadily in towards the blade. Use the left hand to clamp the work, holding it in place over the guide with the thumb.

Take care to keep hands well away from the saw. The left hand will be brought forward of the blade as the work passes through.

For safety, a push stick, a length of scrap timber with a V-cut in one end, should be used instead of the right hand to push the work through for the last section of the cut.

Pushing from both sides closes up the cut around the blade and may cause jamming.

## Cross-cutting
Mark the position of the cut on the material and set the mitre guide at an angle of 45°. Place the work firmly against the mitre gauge, so that the saw cuts just on the waste side of the marked line.

# Jig saws

Start the motor and feed the timber slowly and steadily into the blade. Keep the hands clear of the saw by using them to support the work.

Keep the work firmly against the mitre gauge with the left hand, so that it remains firmly on the table. Hold the waste flat with the right hand.

Always remember that safety is a priority. If any adjustment has to be made, switch off at the socket or remove the plug. If the motor were inadvertently started while you were adjusting the blade, the consequences could be very unpleasant. Always make sure that the saw is switched off before being plugged into the mains and before fitting it on to the saw bench. The blade guard should cover the saw blade, and care should be taken to see that this guard does not become jammed with shavings.

The jig saw is extremely versatile, but as with all power tools care is needed in its use. Always hold the saw firmly, keeping it away from the body. Keep the cable clear of the blade and leave the motor running for a few moments after finishing a cut. Make sure that the tool has stopped before putting your hands near the blade — and preferably first unplug.

If you drop the jig saw, never attempt to catch it. Never use the attachment outside while it is raining or immediately after rain. Store saw blades safely, well away from children and animals.

There are two patterns of integral jig saw, with slightly different switches. One has the conventional switch button which can be locked on; the other an on–off switch. The button is pushed forward into the 'on' position, backwards to the 'off' position.

Check, in particular, that the latter type is switched to 'off' before connecting to the mains. You will get the best results from a jig saw if the work is anchored to a bench or other support.

**Jig saw attachments**
The jig saw attachment is quickly fitted to

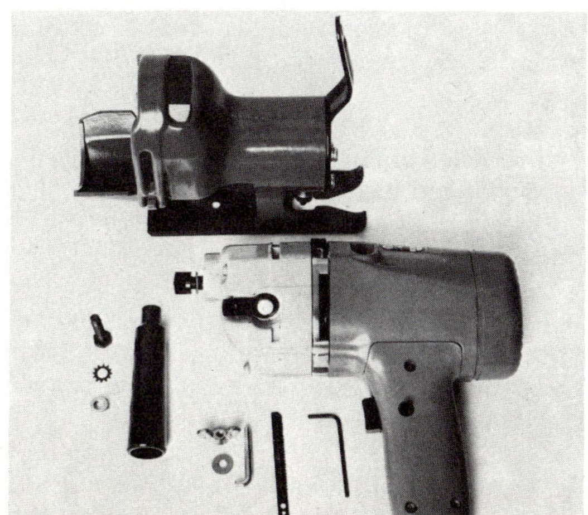

*A jig-saw attachment which fits into the drive shaft of a power drill*

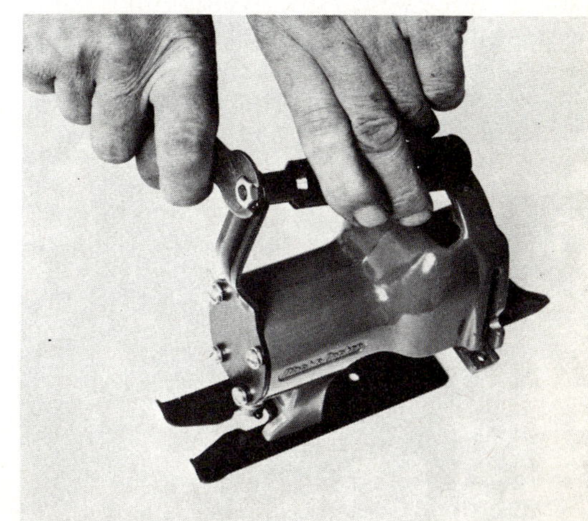

*Assemble the guide handle and eccentric drive attachment to the drill*

a power drill. Fit the handle to the stem with its bolt, spring washer and nut. Remove the drill chuck and fit the drive adaptor into the drive spindle, checking that the washer is in place on the spindle of the adaptor.

Swing open the retaining clamp and inset the nose of the drill into the attachment. Make sure that the drive adaptor is seated correctly in the drive coupling.

Engage the lugs of the casing and clamp in the recess in the drill casing. If you are using a single-speed drill, clamp the attachment with the ventilation slots nearest the nose of the drill.

Close the retaining clamp, ensuring that the lugs are seated in the recesses. Insert

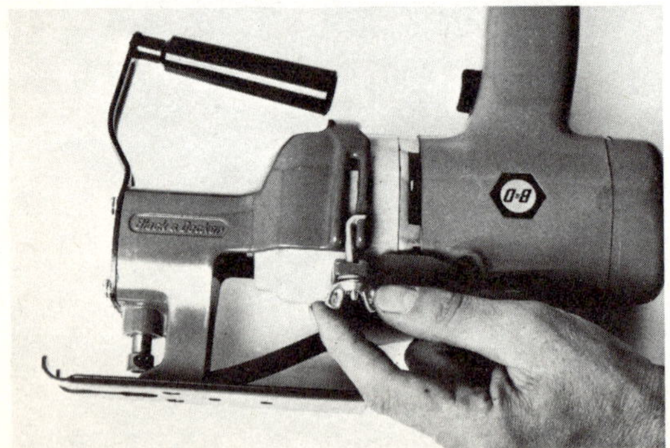

*Wing nut fixes unit to drill body*

the hook bolt into the housing to ensure that the hook section seats into the groove and the threaded end passes through the hole in the retaining clamp. Fit the plain washer and wing nut and screw tight.

When using a two-speed drill normally select the faster speed. You may have to do this before fitting the jig saw attachment, as the drill speed regulator may not be accessible once the attachment is fitted.

With the jig saw attachment a variable-speed drill is able to give finer control of the cut than fixed speeds can give. In other words, it provides a better cutting action over a wide range of materials.

**Blades**
The tool is usually supplied with a general-purpose cutting blade, but there is a variety of blades, which can cut many materials.

In use, cutting blades, which are small and work at high speeds, are placed under considerable stress. Always use a good-quality, sharp blade.

A coarse-toothed blade is used for cutting aluminium and copper, while brass, zinc, plastics and laminate are cut with a fine blade.

Coarse-toothed blades are used for fast cutting of softwood up to 38mm thick and 25mm thick hardwood, blockboard and plywood. A medium blade will cut less quickly but will leave a smoother edge. For thin plywood, where edges may splinter, always use fine-toothed blades. A knife blade cuts paper, soft plastics and rubber.

Before attempting to fit a blade to a jig saw, disconnect the unit from the mains. The same rule applies, of course, when making any adjustment.

The blade is locked in the chuck either by two screws secured by an Allen key, or by a slotted screw, tightened with a screw-driver. Insert the blade with the teeth facing forward. Centralize the blade in the chuck and tighten all set screws against the blade; avoid overtightening.

While jig saw blades are made to cut almost any material, cutting techniques differ for different materials. Make sure that the blade is clear of the bench; cut with scrap material beneath the work if necessary.

**Wood cutting**
Mark the line to be cut on the surface of the work. Straight or curved lines can be followed freehand, as the jig saw has a

built-in blower, so dust does not obscure the line. Air is directed from the drill, through a plastic tube to behind the saw blade.

Large panels of wood must be supported to prevent the saw blade from being pinched by the action of the cut binding together. If the work starts to move or vibrate, stop cutting and secure it properly before resuming.

Start the motor when the shoe is resting firmly on the surface and the blade has not quite reached the place where you stopped cutting. Always let the motor stop before removing a blade from a 'blind' or unfinished cut.

## Pocket cutting

Sometimes you may want to cut a shape out of the middle of a piece of wood. This is called a pocket cut. Mark out the area to be cut. The saw blade can be inserted straight into the surface without drilling a pilot hole.

Tip the saw forward, allowing the rounded tip of the shoe to rest on the surface of the work, keeping the blade well clear.

Switch on the saw, keep the saw at the same angle to the surface and locate the moving blade exactly above the cutting position. With a firm pivoting pressure on the tip of the shoe, and maintaining the blade exactly on the line, lower the rear of the shoe towards the surface.

Once the saw blade has completely entered the wood, and the shoe is resting flat on the surface, the blade can be moved forward along its working line.

A rounded section can be cut in one operation. Several cuts are required to cut a square or oblong. Cut the first side to its fullest extent. With the motor still running, bring the saw back down the cut, curving it gently away from the first cut, to cut the second side. The waste piece left in the corner is cut out later.

Cut the two remaining sides in the same way until most of the waste falls away.

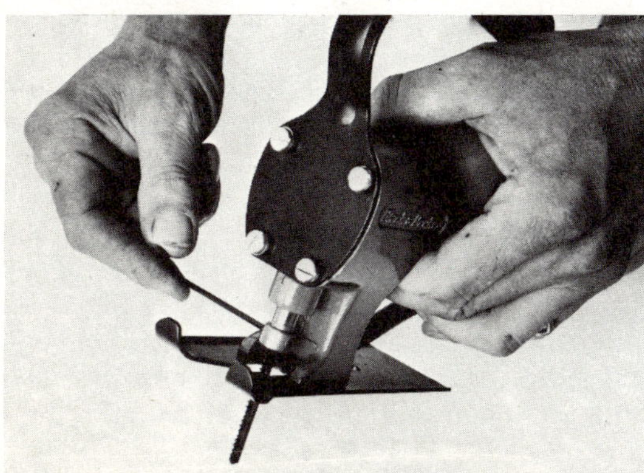

*A wide variety of blades makes the jig saw a highly versatile power tool*

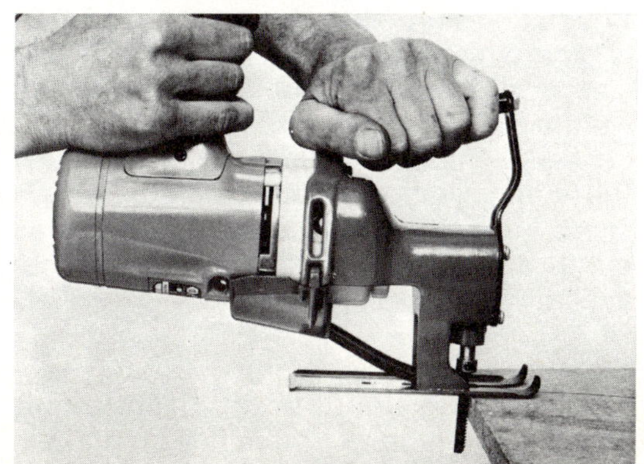

*Rest base plate on the surface when starting a cut at edge of a board*

*Main use of jig saw is to cut angles and curves in various materials*

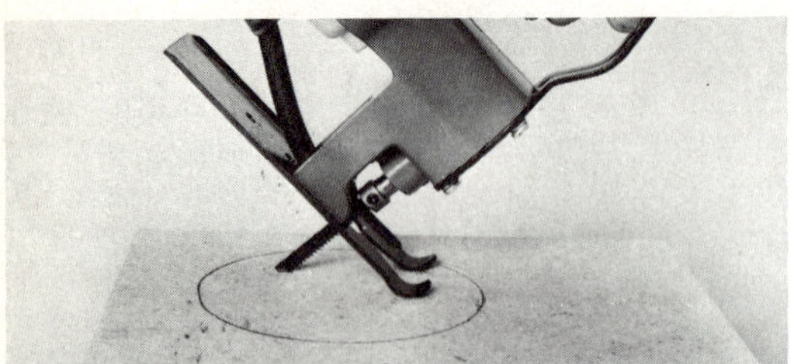

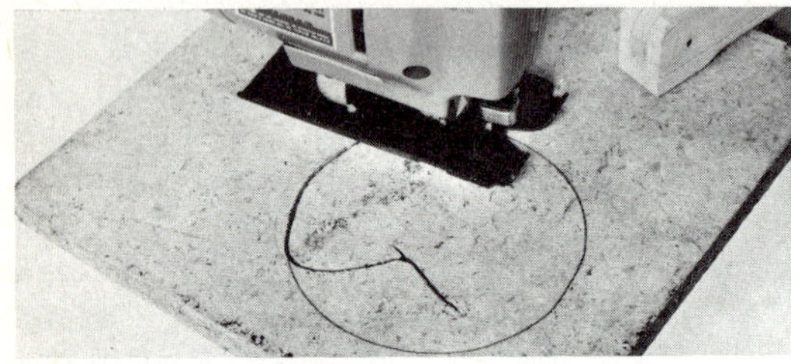

*Start pocket cut in centre, then drop back of unit slowly and cut shape*

Reverse the direction of working, complete the unfinished cuts, then remove the corner pieces.

A small opening, such as a keyhole, can be cut by moving the saw backwards and forwards and taking 'bites' out of the wood.

While the jig saw is not as popular as the circular saw for cutting straight lines, it can be used to do so. To make sure that the line is accurate, nail or clamp a long, straight batten to the work, keeping the shoe pressed firmly against this during cutting.

## Cutting laminates

A fine-toothed metal cutting blade is used here. As wood or plastic laminates are thin, the upstroke of the saw blade may cause splintering on the face of the material nearest to the shoe. To prevent this, place the material face downwards to cut.

To minimize splintering, make a laminate 'sandwich' with hardboard or scrap wood above and below the laminate at the cut line, then cut through the three layers.

## Cutting veneered chipboard

When there are two decorative surfaces, decide which is the main one, place that side face down and cut. To help prevent splintering on the reverse, a problem with veneered chipboard, place sticky tape over the cutting line or score carefully with a sharp knife. Where a curved line is to be cut use several pieces of sticky tape to accommodate the curve.

## Cutting metal

When cutting ferrous sheet and non-ferrous materials, such as copper, aluminium and brass, clamp the sheet on to a backing of softwood or plywood, to prevent vibration and risk of tearing the metal. Spread a thin film of lubricant along the cutting line — oil for steel; paraffin or turpentine on non-ferrous metals — then saw through both sheets.

Damage may be caused to the blade and motor if the blade is forced through the metal. Cutting metal is a slower process than cutting through thick timber — but never force the saw in order to speed up work.

## Cutting plastic sheet

Vinyl plastic sheet can be difficult to cut, for the friction heat may cause the plastic to melt and to fuse solidly behind the blade. Place sticky paper over the line of cut and saw through this. When cutting, use a general-purpose blade.

The protective paper should not be removed until the material has been cut, to avoid scratching the surface.

## Care of jig saws

Always use sharp blades and never allow the motor to run under stress. Signs of stress are immediately apparent; there will be a noticeable reduction in motor speed and the case will start to get warm.

If this happens, remove the saw from the work and run it on 'no load' for a few minutes. The built-in fan will bring the motor back to normal temperature.

Before restarting, check to try to establish the cause of overloading and rectify this.

The saw should be oiled regularly. Use two drops of machine oil, dropped into the oil hole in the side of the tool. Regular checking and servicing are important. The jig saw should be checked after a hundred hours of use or after twelve months, whichever is the sooner.

## Blades of all work

| | Material | Type of cut | Speed of cut | Blade length (mm) |
|---|---|---|---|---|
| | Soft and hardwood | Rough | Fast | 75 |
| | Soft and hardwood, plywood | Medium | Medium | 75 |
| | Soft and hardwood, plywood | Smooth | Medium | 75 |
| | Soft and hardwood, plywood | Smooth | Medium | 100 |
| | Soft and hardwood, plywood | Smooth | Medium | 100 |
| | Plywood | Medium-fine | Medium-fast | 75 |
| | Soft and hardwood, plywood | Smooth | Medium | 100 |
| | Soft and hardwood | Fine | Medium | 63 |
| | Non-ferrous metals | Fine | Slow | 75 |
| | Ferrous (iron) metals | Fine | Slow | 75 |
| | Plywood, plastics | Fine | Medium | 75 |
| | Ferrous (iron) metals | Coarse | Slow | 75 |
| | Leather, rubber compositions (knife edge) | Smooth | Fast | 75 |
| | Wood and plywood | Rough | Fast | 75 |

# Power tool bench

The Workmate is not a power tool, but it can provide a major base for many power tool operations. A big advantage is that the bench can be taken to the work, invaluable when using power tools around the home. There is both a single- and a dual-height version of the light-weight Workmate, though the single height version is now no longer made. You can use the dual-height version at single height; extra legs snap out to increase the height. The unit folds flat and can be hung on a garage or workshop wall out of the way — a great space-saver.

The Workmate contains in its work top perhaps the biggest vice in the world — it measures a giant 740mm long and has a 100mm opening. Power tools and attachments can be used on the bench by mounting them firmly on a baseboard, screwed to a batten, clamped within the bench's vice bars.

A range of attachments for the Workmate increases its versatility when used with power tools. Metal vice claddings have been designed to fit over the wood vice work top and protect the surfaces.

Universal extender arms allow large pieces of material to be placed on the unit, making them more manageable when using power tools.

*Workmate fitted with extension arms*

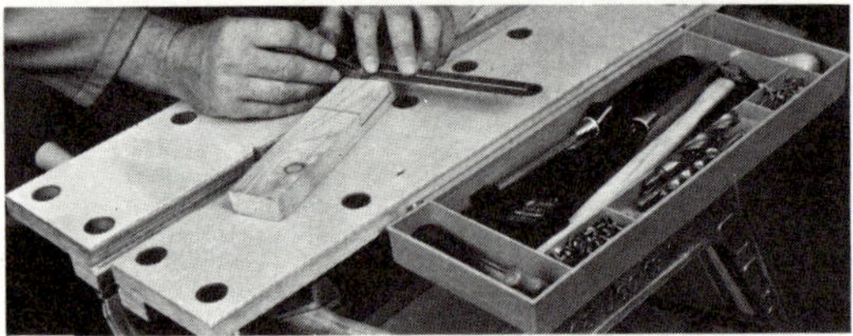

*Bench with the detachable tool tray*

These can be positioned in any of the seven holes in the arm and into the various holes in the vice top, giving great flexibility in use. Large sheets of wood can be held, using the arms, while making cuts with a circular saw (not the jig saw). The arms also allow corner clamping of material.

A removable tool tray can be attached to the Workmate. This is useful for holding power tool accessories, steel tapes and other tools.

A saw table — suitable for use with the

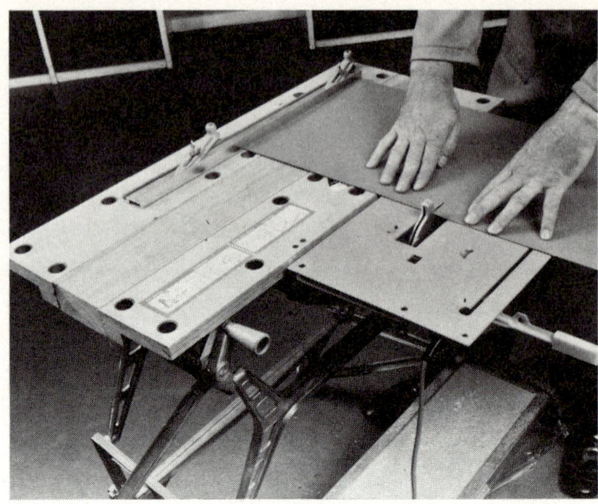

*Saw-bench attachment, with optional rip guide fence, may be fitted*

Workmate — enables the Workmate to be used as a versatile saw bench. A mounting bracket is first fixed to the bench, but the saw table and saw are removable and the assembled unit saw bench merely slots into place. It is intended for use with any Black & Decker portable saw or saw attachment.

The metal bench top enables the usual saw cuts to be made and incorporates a rip fence and mitre guide. A supplementary rip fence, which fits into the Workmate vice-jaws, allows a substantially wider cut to be made than when using the ordinary saw table.

# Making joints

**Tenons**

To cut a tenon on a saw bench, first cross-cut the timber to length, and make sure that the ends are square. One of two methods may be used, though the first may be less satisfactory than the second in some circumstances.

*Rebates can be cut on saw bench. Mark cut and set blade to depth*

*Set depths carefully; the second saw pass completes the rebate*

There is a limit to the depth of cut that can be made with a power saw; it may not be possible to saw deeply enough on the horizontal cut and, if you are using long timbers, it may not be possible to hold them sufficiently steady. Very long timbers might even be too tall for your workshop area.

In the first method, which is preferable, only horizontal cuts are made. Adjust the saw to the depth of the tenon, clamping a batten to the bench as a guide. Make the first cut right on the shoulder. Hold the work lightly against the guide as it is pushed across.

Feed the work into the saw to make a series of further cross-cuts, and complete the joint without a vertical cut. For the repetition cross-cuts there is no need to follow a line. Lap joints can also be cut by this method.

The second method of squaring the ends up is carried out as follows. Make two saw cuts, one vertical and one horizontal, for each shoulder. When making the vertical cut, hold the work upright and firmly against the fence with the left hand. Use a push-stick in the right hand to drive the work towards the saw.

Turn the work on its side and make a cross-cut to complete the shoulder. A rip fence is not normally necessary on cross-cuts, other than for small jobs such as this, where it is quite safe not to use the fence.

As two settings of both the rip fence and saw are needed to make the tenon, you can speed up work in repetition cutting if you first make all the vertical cuts before changing over to the horizontal setting.

The corresponding mortise may be cut using a power drill and suitable wood-

*Kerfed timber has series of close grooves cut on back so that it can be curved*

working bit in a vertical drill stand. This is described later in the chapter.

**Cutting a rebate or ploughing a groove**

Mark, on the timber, the depth of cut required. Place the timber on the bench and adjust the depth of cut on the saw blade.

**Kerfing**

Kerfing is a technique which allows you to bend or curve an otherwise straight piece of timber or plywood. It consists of a series of parallel slots, cut with the saw, across the inside surface of the timber, which enables it to be bent in a curve without snapping.

Adjust the saw cut depth to nine-tenths of the depth of the timber, that is all but one layer, in the case of plywood. Establish the extent of the curve. Mark the back of the wood to show the position of the curve. The tighter the curve, the closer the number of saw cuts along that portion.

Make the first cut along the right-hand line, sighting the position of the cut through the saw slot — a similar method to that used in making a housing joint.

*Neat tenon joints can be cut on the saw bench by making several passes*

Place the inside edge of the saw slot on this first cut when you make the second cut, to provide an indication of the spacing of each cut. The number of cuts can be adjusted as you work to get the required radius of the kerf.

If two identical pieces of kerfed timber are required with the same radius, rather than cutting each separately, it is easier to cut both in one operation. Use a piece of timber of twice the width, cut the kerfing lines and then rip-saw down the middle.

Applications for kerfed timber include making the front of a curved bar or a rounded end of a kitchen corner unit.

## Housing joints

The cutting of most types of joint requires the use of a saw table, but simple joints, such as the housing joint, can be cut with a portable circular saw. Mark a line with a try-square on the piece of timber to indicate one edge of the joint.

Place a scrap piece of wood accurately on the marked line, then draw the other edge of the joint. Adjust the depth of cut to half that of the timber. The piece of scrap timber is held against the far side of the work, to stop 'whiskering'; cut slightly inside both lines.

When cutting on the right, sight through the saw slot to ensure that the outer edge of the blade comes just inside the line. For cuts from the left side, sight through the notch at the front. This is to make sure that the inside edge of the blade is just within the waste.

Finally, make a series of parallel cuts across the waste, snapping off the projecting tongues with a chisel, held sideways; then clean out the bottom of the joint with the chisel.

## Cutting a mortise

To cut the corresponding mortise slot fit a suitable drill bit into a drill mounted in a vertical drill stand, cut a series of adjacent holes, and finish off the slot with a woodworking chisel. It is essential to mount the drill in the stand to make the initial holes in timber, for you cannot drill to the necessary precision with a hand-held power drill.

The base of the stand allows you to fix your own jig, or you can use the drill stand vice. You can make a jig from an offcut of blockboard or plywood, with a

*To cut matching mortise, drill line of holes*

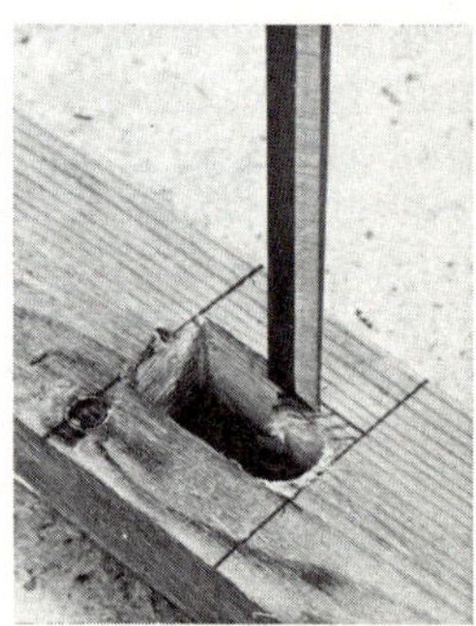

*Next, square off the holes using a chisel*

piece of softwood to provide a shoulder at the back which acts as a stop.

Mark out the mortise to width and length, using a try-square and marking knife for the length and a mortise gauge for the width. Fix it into the jig or drill vice and set the drill carriage at the correct height on the column.

Establish the depth of the mortise and mark this on a drill bit. Use a drill bit the width of the mortise. Measure from the cutting edges of the bit and not from the spike. Wrap a length of adhesive tape around the drill in a clockwise direction from the cutting end; this ensures it does not unwind in use. You can also use a plastic depth stop, fitted as standard to some drills.

Once you have set everything up, locate the cradle so that the point of the bit is 13mm away from the work, switch on, and pull down the operating handle with a steady, even pressure. The positive control of the drill operation helps to prevent 'snatching' on break-through. The note of the motor will ease on break-through; at that point, ease off the pressure.

Drill the first hole, then move the work along, to drill the next hole alongside. Repeat this for the length of the mortise.

All you will be left with is a small amount to square off on the sides and at the corners.

You can drill into the end of a long piece of timber by placing the wood vertically on the flooring and swinging out the cradle or carriage clear of the bench. Prop the wood firmly in position when drilling.

**Router**
A router is a fast-moving tool — it works at an unreduced speed of 30,000 rpm, direct from its electric motor. This high speed is important to produce fine cutting work.

This purpose-designed tool can cut a considerable range of profiles in timber, using the appropriate bits; it can also be used for slotting and grooving, using its detachable edge guide to guide the tool accurately along the timber edge.

Using other accessories, you can cut accurate shapes and profiles from timber. The tool has a very wide application in cutting specialized shapes, such as beading profiles.

The router is operated by a trigger in the handle. You can hold this on to run continuously by depressing a lock-on button, as with various other tools, and the lock is disengaged simply by squeezing the trigger.

When using the router, it is most important to hold its base firmly flat on to the surface, moving the tool from left to right when straight cutting at a rate that maintains a high motor speed. For irregular or circular

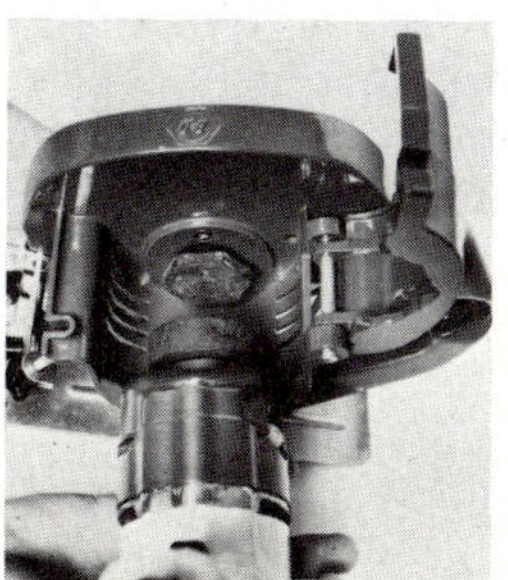

*The integral router revolves at 30,000 rpm*

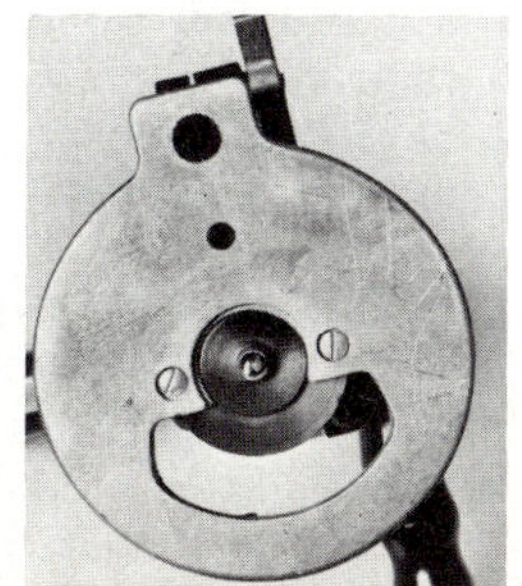

*Flat base plate, showing cutter spindle*

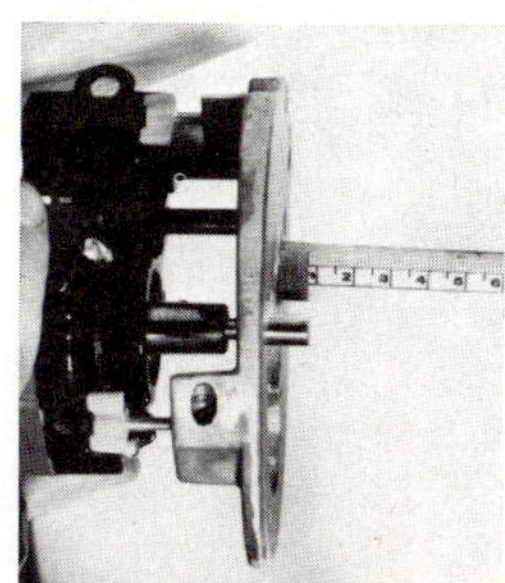

*Depth of cut can be measured, then set*

*Unit can be used freehand to cut shapes*

cutting, move the router counter-clockwise.

Operating the router too slowly may cause the bit to burn the wood, while feeding too fast can quickly cause undue wear on the bit — and also produce an inferior cut. As wood densities vary, it is not possible to give exact feeding speeds. The best way is to practise using the router on different pieces of timber, as you will then acquire the 'feel' of the tool for the correct feeding speed.

Generally, it is good practice to make trial cuts on a scrap piece of wood before attempting to carry out the finished project.

As a general rule, the maximum cut with any one pass should be no more than 3mm—4mm in depth, dependent on the diameter of the bit. Make sure when fitting the cutters that the flat on the bit lines up with the bit-holding grub screw, and ensure that this is tight. After making any adjustments make sure that all wing nuts and screws are firmly tightened.

## Edge guide
You can cut circles with the router using the edge guide. This is assembled upside down on the front of the tool with a standard, 11-gauge nail, 63mm long, set into the hole in the front of the guide, hammered into the material to a depth of about 6mm to form a pivot point. Circles ranging from a minimum of 125mm diameter to a maximum of 300mm diameter can be cut out, by adjusting the set of the edge guide.

Standard items with the router are an edged circular guide, a 6mm cutter bit, and an Allen key for bit changing.

## Fitting the router bit
Loosen the grub screw with its Allen key and insert the bit with the flat edge towards the grub screw hold. Tighten the screw against the flat surface of the cutting bit to hold it securely.

## Fixtures and attachments
There is a wide range of fixtures and attachments you can use with the router. These include a slot- and circle-cutting attachment, general-purpose template guides, a full range of router bits up to 19mm capacity, 'V' groove bits, beading bits, straight bits, veining bits, core-box bits and chamfering bits.

## Dowelling jig
A dowel joint is both strong and neat. A dowelling jig, used with a power drill, enables this type of joint to be made with precision and speed.

This jig, made by Record Tools, is

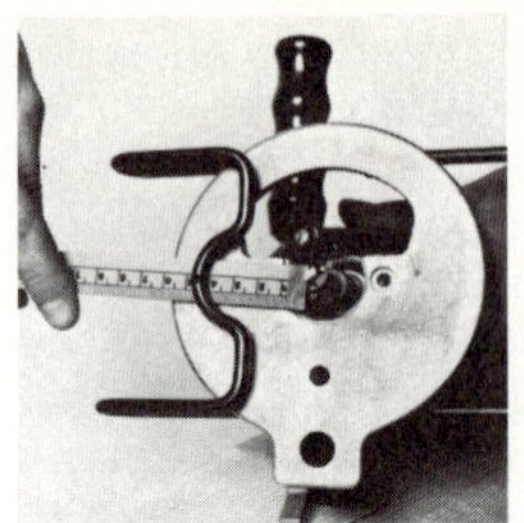

*Measuring lateral adjustment using guide*

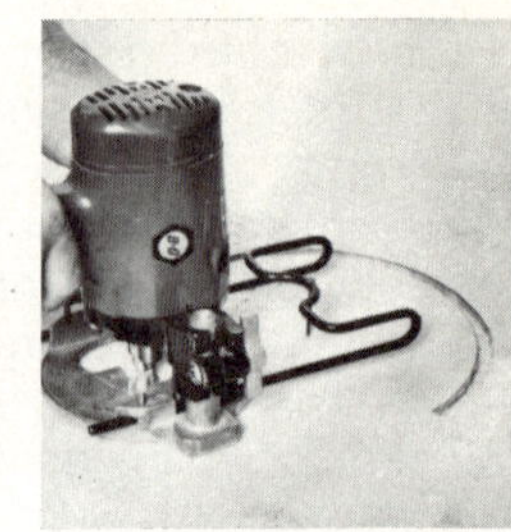

*Circles cut using guide located on pin*

*Screw-on handle aids control without guide. Depth setting is on left*

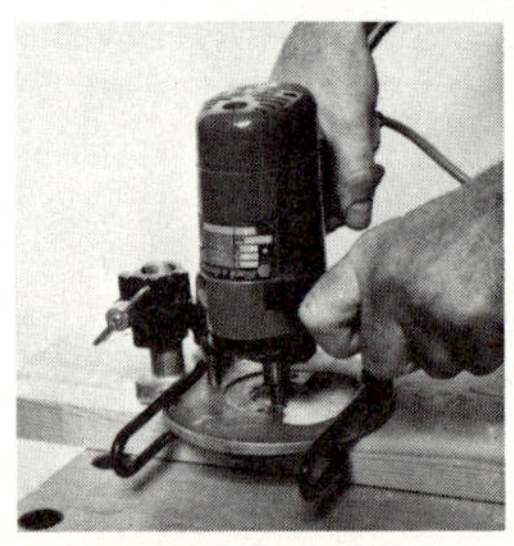

*Using the guide for lateral milling*

*Home-made edge guides give greater control*

intended to use 6mm, 8mm or 9·5mm dowels. The principle of the jig is to drill two matching holes, insert a section of dowel into one, then joint this to the matching hole.

The jig consists of two hardened steel bushes held in carriers fitted with double fences and mounted on slide rods so that you can set the distance between dowel holes.

An adjustable head can be fixed in any position along the rods and carries two screws fitted with nylon swivel shoes so that the jig can be clamped securely to the work.

Some ten types of joint can be made in framing, carcassing and board jointing. In framing, corner, T-mitre and leg joints can

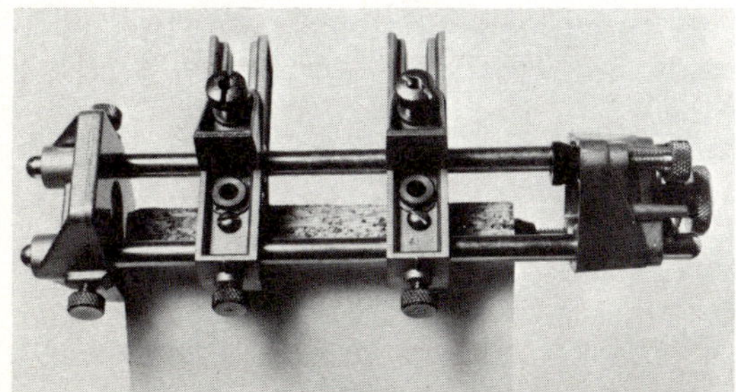

*The jig is set up at an angle when carrying out carcass mitre cutting*

be made in timber of a minimum thickness of 16mm and a maximum thickness of 76mm.

Carcass jointing — making corner joints, shelving and mitre joints and holes for adjustable shelving — can be made in various widths of timber but using suitable slide rods from the range available.

For 152mm-wide boards, you use standard rods; for boards 305mm wide, medium rods; and for 460mm boards, long slide rods.

Three types of board jointing are possible — end to end, edge to edge, and edge clamping.

No complicated marking out is needed for any joint. Bush positions are simply set using a rule and measuring from the unit's reference head to the bush-carrier datum line — and also from the fence face to the bush-carrier datum.

When preparing boards, a line must be squared across the board to show the position of the line of dowels so that the jig can be lined up accurately.

A similar line is necessary for correct position of the bush carrier when making T-joints.

To drill the opposite member of a joint, the jig is simply inverted. Bush positions should not be altered until all the related holes have been drilled.

Wood twist bits are used to drill holes with a power drill, working at a maximum speed. Cut all dowels to equal length, but slightly shorter than the total depth of both holes, to ensure a flush fit to the joint and perfect mating when assembled.

Chamfer the ends of the dowels, as this will ensure an easy fit into the dowel holes.

Before inserting the dowels, place wood-working adhesive into the holes. Make a

*Piece of dowel inserted through the drill bush into the hole provides a reference point*

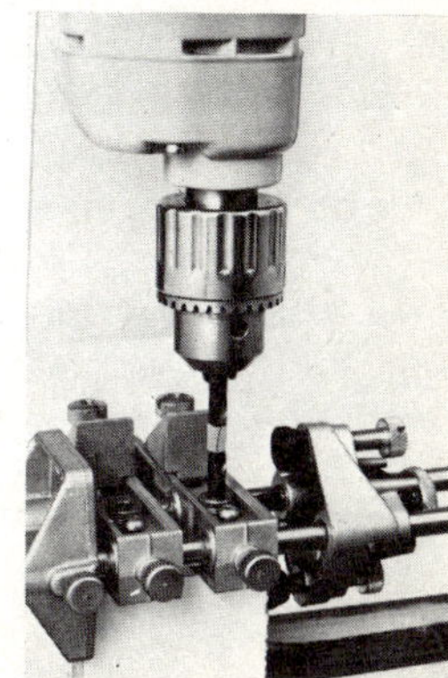

*Check when inverting jig that reference head and fences are against marked faces*

*Joint is completed; it is fully knocked together*

saw cut along the length of the dowel, as this groove will allow both end and excess glue to be squeezed out.

A depth gauge can be formed by placing a piece of insulating tape on the drill, level with the bush carrier, first inserting the drill through the bush to the depth required.

The jig is straightforward to assemble and additional 8mm bushes and 305mm and 460mm rods are available as accessories.

## Comb-jointing attachment
The comb joint is one of the most attractive woodwork joints — a strong joint, calling for skill and considerable precision if made with hand tools.

A comb-jointing attachment fitted to a power drill incorporates this precision skill in the actual tool. Carefully set up and used, you can short-circuit possibly years of practice to produce joints indistinguishable from those of the master craftsman — and made a lot more quickly.

One of the major uses of this strong joint is for assembling sections of drawers, which must go together with precision if they are not to jam or bind and simply not to fit.

## Assembly
Screw the horizontal bench stand firmly to the workbench or a blockboard base. Remove the chuck and fit the drill to the bench stand. Set the drill to run at the fast speed.

Use the two supplied hook bolts and wing nuts to attach the table-mounting bracket to the bench stand. An adaptor plate and round-head engineer's screws are used for fitting older, pressed-metal stands.

Fit the arbor to the drill spindle. Mount the saw blade, fitting the bevelled 'wobble' washers, and check that the direction of rotation is correct. The plain unstamped

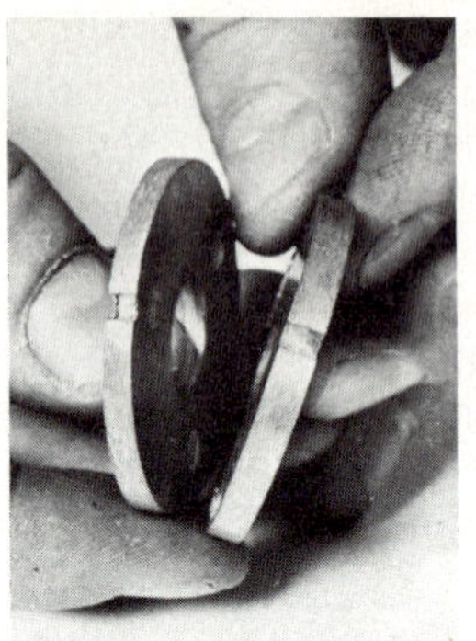

*Bevelled washers, lined up with edge slots, fitted on each side of blade*

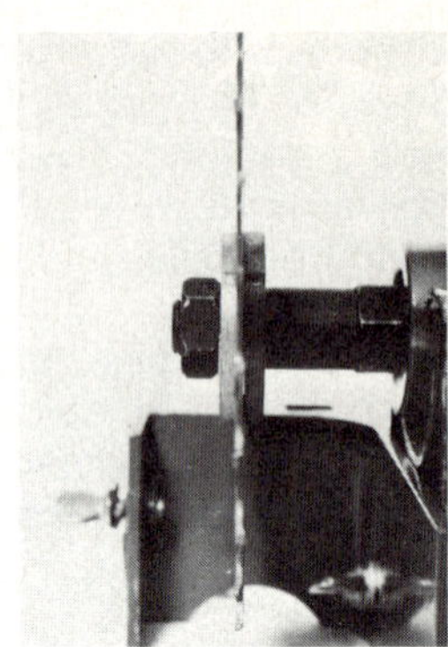

*Saw arbor fitted to drill. Blade 'wobbles' to give width of comb joint*

side should be next to the blade.

Line up the notch marks on the wobble washers so that one thick and one thin side are aligned, then tighten the saw blade securing nut. Use two spanners to obtain the correct blade tightness — one holds the arbor, the other secures the nut.

After tightening, recheck that the notch marks remain correctly aligned.

Next, fit the jointer table assembly. Locate the pillar in the vertical hole of the mounting bracket so the saw is opposite the wood insert which is part of the table. Set the height of the table so that the centre line or the wood to be combed points to

*Align edge of table with saw teeth*

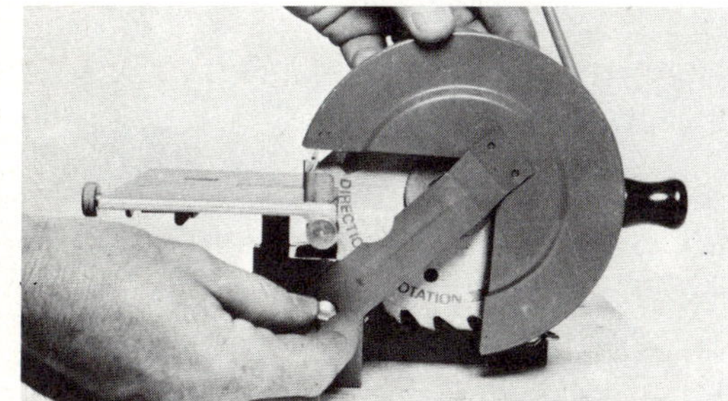

*Line up wood with centre of saw blade*

the centre of the saw blade.

The radius formed by the saw cut is then equalized over the thickness of the wood, giving a square joint. Tighten the thumb screw. When using timber of varying thickness it will be necessary to reset the height of the table. This does not matter with thin material.

To position the tips of the saw blade teeth, use a straight-edged piece of wood as a guide. Place this on the table firmly against the lipped front edge.

Unscrew the wing nuts securing the bracket by one or two turns, and adjust the bracket table sub-assembly until the true edge just touches the blade tips. Retighten the wing nuts evenly.

The hook bolts must maintain their position in the drill stand. Finally, recheck the edge-to-blade tip adjustment.

To save time, mark the position of the bracket, in relation to the bench stand, for reference. Further adjustment should be

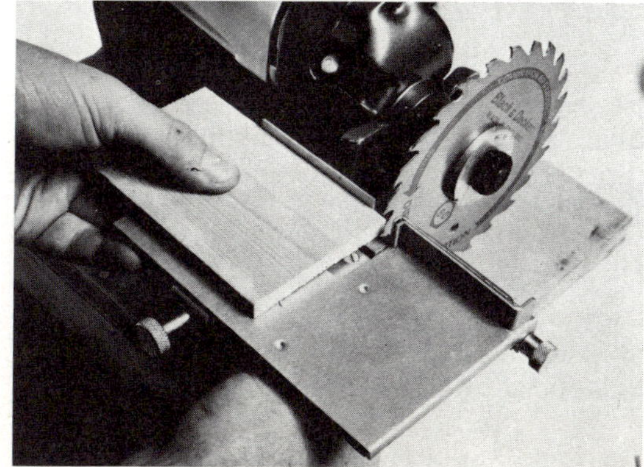

*Use scrap to adjust for thickness. Adjust exactly when aligning blade*

necessary only when the blade is removed or shows signs of wear.

The wood insert in the table helps to reduce fraying on the underside of the cut. It is correctly adjusted when a small saw cut is produced when the tool is first switched on. Over-adjusting the setting may result in a jamming blade.

To adjust the wood insert so that it remains close up to the blade, slightly loosen the fixing screw, then, with a piece of waste wood, gently tap forward from below until the saw just touches the top edge. Retighten the screw.

It may be necessary to sand the surface of a replacement insert until it is level with the table slide surface.

Attach the saw guard to the end of the bracket. Check that all the fixings are tightened and that the saw blade is rotating freely inside the guard.

Unscrew the depth-adjusting screw on the front of the table for about 13mm, and place a piece of square-ended waste wood on the slide with the end grain to the saw and its right-hand edge against the register lip to the right of the wood insert.

Switch on, and with the saw running push

the wood and platform towards the saw to make a cut of about 10mm in depth. Always hold the work with the hands well clear of the saw.

Switch off the saw, unplug the drill and loosen the screw that clamps the two register plates together. Place the saw cut over the register lips, then open them to fit the cut comfortably, and retighten the clamping screw.

The function of the two registers, once adjusted, is to locate the work positively to give accurate spacing.

Examine the cut to see that the arc of the saw is equalized over the thickness of the wood, and adjust the table height if necessary.

Next, compare the distance of the cut from the edge of the wood with the width of the cut. If the tenon is wider than the cut, turn the adjusting screw on the right-hand front corner of the slide to move both registers bodily towards the saw; adjust in the other direction if too narrow. Test by taking similar cuts on two pieces of waste wood and fitting the two cut tenons together.

*Set unit to fast speed, cut trial slots; check that arc of cut is even*

A comfortable fit with two tenons will generally give a considerably tighter fit over a larger number; in hardwood, a slightly looser fit is necessary than in softwood.

Once this adjustment has been made there should be no need to alter it unless the set of the saw teeth diminishes for any reason, or you use different materials.

Do not alter this setting while making a joint, but always obtain the fit required by first testing on waste wood.

*Adjust guide to set out width to match the distance from edge of wood*

The depth screw controls the depth of the cut. This must always be equal to the thickness of the piece to be fitted to that being combed. The mating piece is placed edgeways between the head of the screw and the table and the screw tightened on to it.

You can allow a little play so that the tenons when assembled will protrude for sanding smooth, as this produces a cleaner finish.

*Check that the trial sets correspond*

*Once correct, make final comb cuts*

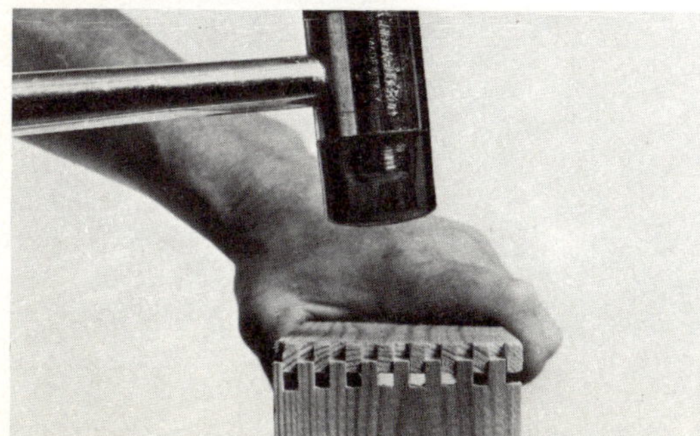
*Tap joints together, using soft hammer*

Use a smooth, steady, even movement towards the saw, as a sharp movement may cause the saw cut to very. It is wise to practise this initially on scrap timber.

## Making a comb joint
A single joint will rarely be needed but making this will help you to become familiar with the action of the jointer — particularly with the adjustment of the depth stop to give different thicknesses in the same joint.

Take two pieces of wood of equal width and use one piece to adjust the depth stop. Place the second piece on the slide, with the end grain to the saw and the face edge against the left-hand side of the register.

Advance the wood and slide towards the saw until the stop is reached, place the cut obtained over the two register lips and cut again. Repeat this until the left side of the wood clears the saw.

Use the piece of wood you have just combed to readjust the depth stop, if the two pieces are of different thickness. Place this piece on the slide, but turn it side over side with the cut first made over the lips of the register.

Hold this firmly in position and use its left edge as the register to make the first cut on the third piece, and then complete combing the end as previously.

Turn the third piece end over end and comb its second end. Comb both ends of the fourth piece in exactly the same way as the third.

The sides may be knocked together using a block and mallet or a soft hammer, or put together using a clamp or vice. If the tongues are cut slightly over-length for sanding smooth after assembly, use a piece of combing of the same gauge, preferably in hardwood, placed over the joint when assembling the sections, so that the tongues can protrude.

Allow for this when cutting out the sides and adjust the depth stop to allow for differing thicknesses.

The saw must be kept sharp to get the best results, and the wood insert block must always be correctly adjusted.

Always hold the work so that your fingers are at the back edge of the platform, well clear of the saw.

## Milling table
The milling table is designed for use with a power drill and vertical drill stand. This

combination, together with the mill-cutters, forms a vertical milling unit. It can be used for grooving and rebating, and for producing a wide range of precision wood cuts, including mouldings.

The base of the milling table is metal with two straight slits in it. This is fixed to the base of the drill stand with two sets of nuts, bolts and washers.

The base is correctly positioned when the small hole in it is directly aligned with the tip of a normal drill bit.

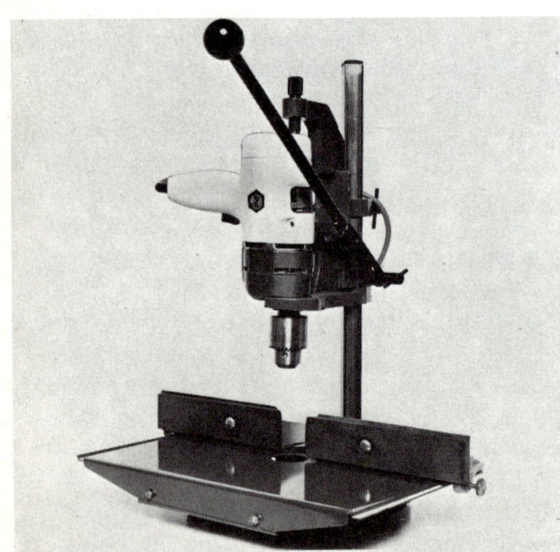

*Milling table is set up on drill stand*

Next, screw the four hexagonal screws with washers loosely into the threads of the milling table base. The work-top surface, the large metal part with a large circular hole, fits over the base.

Check that the washers are on the outside of the screw and then tighten them firmly to fix the working surface to the base.

Fit the guide so that it runs in the tracks on either side of the working surface. Insert locking screws at each side, tightening them to lock the guide in position.

Next, fit the two adjustable wooden guides. These enable you to increase or decrease the amount of cutting bit that protrudes, and they are fitted so that the angled ends locate over the central hole in the working surface.

The gap between the guide should be kept to the minimum necessary for the particular job. This ensures that the timber moves steadily across the cutter.

Before starting on the finished work, run a test on a sample piece of wood to check that the cutting depth is correct. When using a multi-speed drill select the highest speed.

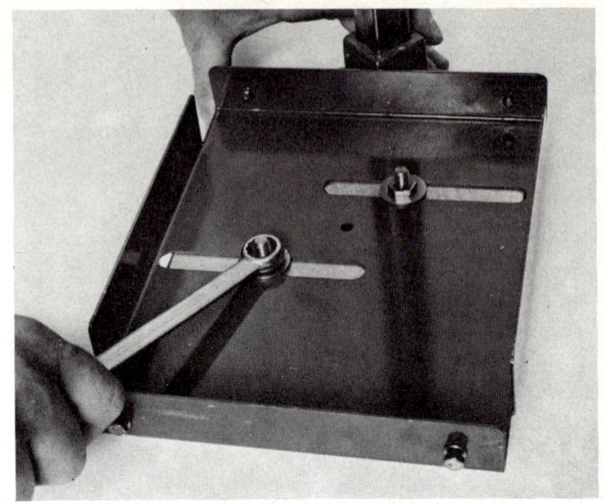

*Milling table base is fitted to the drill stand with nuts and washers*

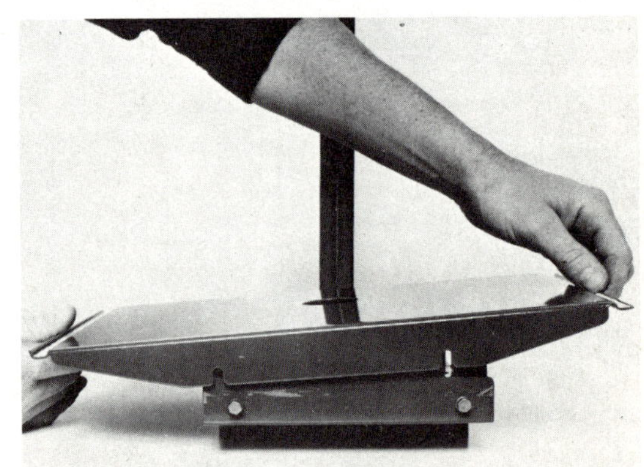

*Locate base so tip of standard drill bit lines up with holes in base*

*Adjustable guides with angled ends locate on central hole in work surface*

Three cutters are provided with the Black & Decker milling table, but you can use a wide range of extra cutters and other accessories. These include slotting cutters of varying sizes, a grooving cutter, a 45° chamfer cutter, a laminate trimmer and a depth stop for use with the drill stand.

Always disconnect the drill from the power supply before assembling, adjusting or detaching the unit, and keep your hands well away from the cutters when using the milling table.

*Fences are adjustable so that depth of cut can be measured accurately*

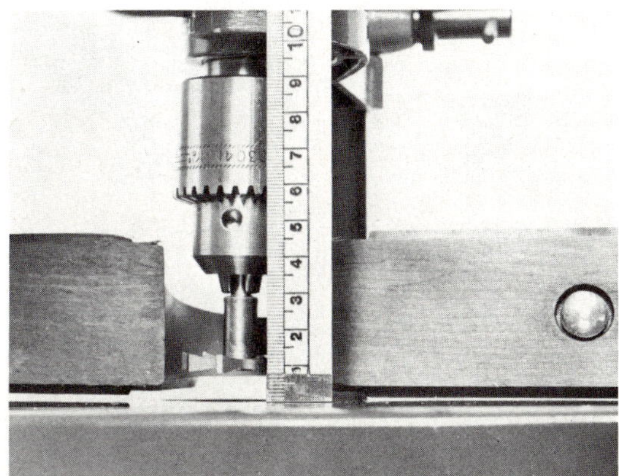

*Measure for height, then set depth stop to correspond on drill*

*Slot cutting. Always hold the work firmly against the fence*

*Groove cutting. Chamfer cutter and laminate trimmer are other cutters*

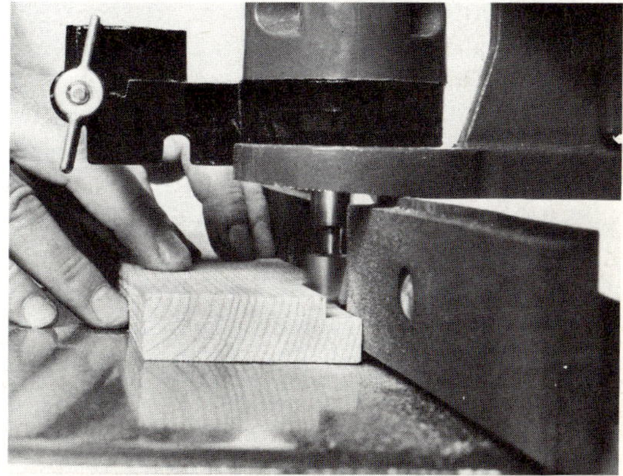

*Rebate cuts can also be made; various routing operations can be achieved*

# Woodworking attachments

The multi-purpose woodworking attachment, supplied with three cutters, fits into the head of the drill after the chuck is removed.

Another name for this type of attachment is a rabeter or rebate attachment. The three supplied cutters enable you to slot, groove, mill, trim or bevel. A full range of cutters consists of three slotting cutters, a grooving and a chamfer cutter and a laminate trimmer.

With this attachment, you can work on ready assembled pieces, such as door and window frames, in a way not possible using a milling table.

Before fitting the attachment to the drill, make sure that the latter is disconnected from the mains. Once screwed in place on the drill, the shaft of the attachment is tightened with a supplied hexagonal key. When fitting this, make sure that the attachment's handle is on the same side as the handle of the drill.

Vertical and horizontal adjustments are made by loosing adjustment knobs which set both height and depth. To make a vertical adjustment, loosen the central adjustment knob, which allows the attachment to slide down on its shaft to produce the desired setting.

*Multi-purpose woodworking attachment screws into drive shaft of drill*

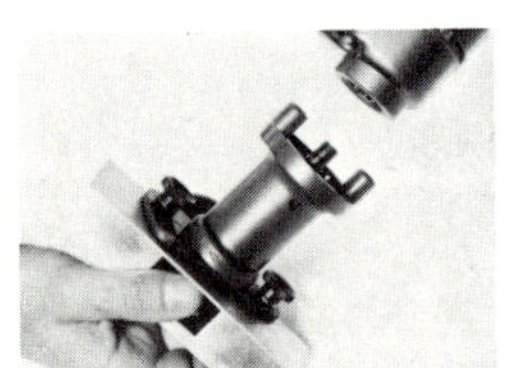

*Lugs ensure accurate alignment of attachment*

*Tighten shaft to attachment with Allen key*

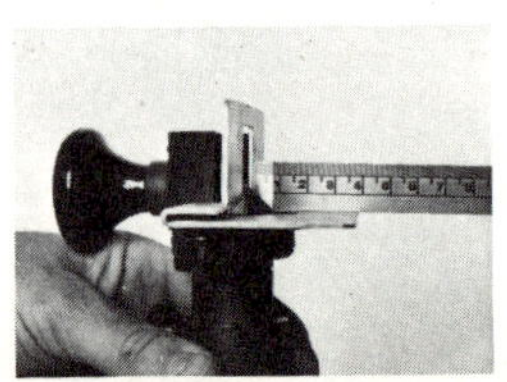

*Vertical adjustment is made on central knob*

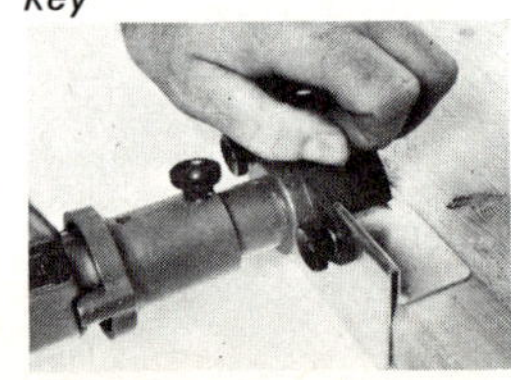

*The edge guide ensures accurate cutting work*

Horizontal adjustment is set by raising or lowering the pivoted guard to the required depth.

With multi-speed drills, use the higher speed. Make sure that any hammer attachment is disengaged before use.

To obtain consistently good results, the attachment should be used only with light pressure, as this will avoid jamming and causing the bits to overheat.

When fitting a cutter, make sure that the cutting edges of the bit follow the arrow on the guard of the attachment, which shows the direction in which the shaft revolves.

To fit or change cutters, lock the shaft of the attachment, or it will not turn when you attempt to remove cutters. First unplug the drill, then insert the stop bar (supplied with the attachment) through the hole on the underside of the attachment housing and through the locating hole in the shaft inside the housing. Loosen the hexagonal screw with the hexagonal key. You can now fit the cutter.

# Wood-turning lathe

Wood-turning is a satisfying pursuit. There are many things you can make, from simple egg-cups to large bowls. You may turn more elaborate objects, such as chair legs and mouldings, and even make chess men.

A wood-turning lathe used with a power drill can even be turned to profit, for you could turn items to sell.

A lathe attachment consists of a steel channel with two parallel rails forming the bed of the lathe. Attached to it is a fixed headstock section — which is usually the horizontal drill stand, so this attachment is a dual-purpose one.

**Setting up**
The bed of the lathe should be firmly mounted to a bench, or to a baseboard that can be mounted or locked in a vice, for considerable vibration may be set up when using the lathe.

The headstock is at one end of the lathe, and the T-bar tool rest and tailstock at the other end bolt to the rails of the lathe bed. The tailstock is adjustable for position, and slides up or down according to length of the timber you are turning. It is also the end bearing for the timber in the lathe.

A power drill is used to drive the lathe and

fixes in the headstock; it slots into a collar and a backscrew tightens to lock it firmly in place. There are two forms of work: turning between centres, in which the piece being turned is secured between head- and tailstocks, and turning on the face-plate.

You must first remove the chuck from the drill and screw in a lathe-driving dog for turning between centres, or else attach a face-plate, for face-plate turning, to the spindle.

For turning between centres, the wood is held between two steel pins or 'dogs', one at each end. These are called the 'driving centre' and the 'tail centre'.

The dogs impress into the wood and keep it centred when spinning. The T-bar rest can be slid along and locked into any position to give the correct height and position to support the cutting tool.

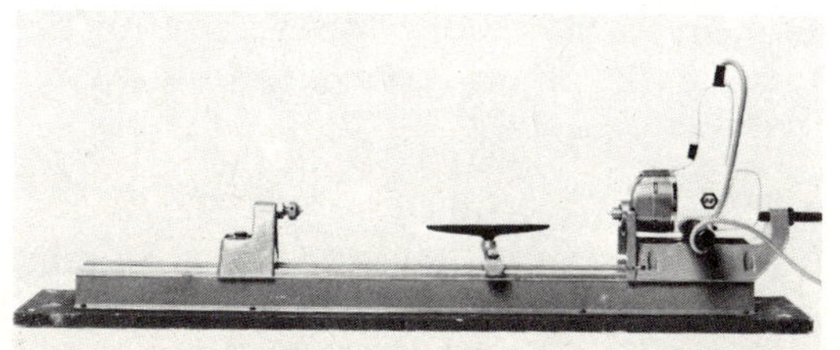

*Wood-turning lathe uses power drill*

Face-plate turning is used for turning round objects, such as bowls and lamp-stand bases.

Another attachment is the screw-point chuck, also called an egg-cup chuck. This is used to hold small articles by a single woodscrew through the centre, with a set-screw at the back to fasten the face-plate to the drill spindle, which you adjust with an Allen key.

A multi-speed drill is best for wood-turning. For large pieces, use slower speeds. Higher speeds can be used for smaller objects. The best results are obtained by using hardwood.

There is no virtue in cutting for the sake of it. Squared pieces of wood would tend to vibrate and judder if you attempted to round them off with lathe tools, and the wood-turning tool might be jerked out of your hand.

It is best to shape rounded objects first roughly with a chisel or a plane to an octagonal section.

To set up a timber blank for turning between centres, mark the centres diagonally at each end, so that you get a true centre. Allow about 25mm of waste, for you will separate this at the end of turning

*When face-plate turning, drill out as much waste as possible to cut work*

with a chisel called a parting tool. Make sure that the ends are square and flat.

Make a small dent in the middle of the piece of timber at each end, using one of the lathe dogs, to provide purchase for both head and tail dogs.

Grease the tailstock with candle wax as this keeps the timber from heating at the tailstock end.

## Turning between centres

It is ambitious to suppose that you will turn out first-class work at a first attempt. It is wiser to carry out a fair amount of practice. A broomstick is a good item to start with; you can practise cutting various ornamentations on it.

Screw the driving or headstock dog into the spindle and slide along the tailstock until it supports the blank between the centres. Make sure that both dogs are accurately engaged in the prepared holes, or the wood will turn off-centre and be difficult to shape accurately.

Tighten in the tailstock dog with its Allen key, then, holding the key in one of the tightening holes, tighten the base clamp with the spanner to lock the tailstock firmly into the lathe bed. Avoid over-tightening as this may cause the end to heat up. You can now give the unit a trial spin to see that it revolves freely and squarely.

Set the rest at about 3mm below the centre line of the work and the same distance away from it. Before starting up, make sure that you have no loose items of clothing or long hair that could catch in the revolving wood or any moving parts.

Check that the wood turns squarely and does not catch on the tool rest or on the body of the lathe. Lock the drill on for continuous running.

## Wood-turning tools

There are two main types of wood-turning tool: those used for cutting and those used for scraping. The tools are hand-held and supported on the tool rest while turning.

The basic tools are the gouge and the chisel. Concave sections are cut with gouges; convex sections with chisels. Square shoulders are cut with parting tools or chisels, and beads with chisels.

*Cutting tools*

Chisels and gouges are cutting tools. Chisels are used for finishing work. The standard chisel is made in sizes of 13mm, 19mm and 25mm. The edge may be

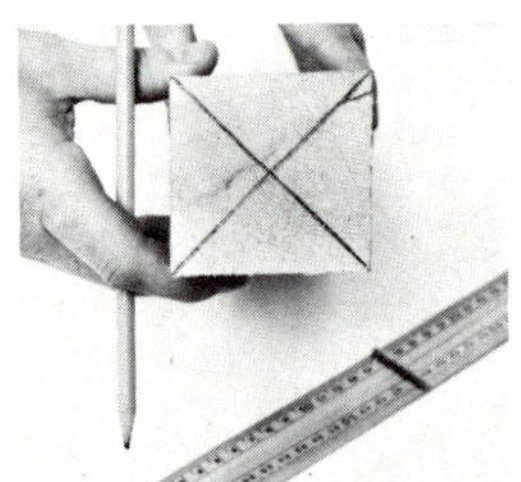

*Cross-mark to find centre of piece of timber to be turned*

*Tap head and tail stock 'dogs' in centres to leave fixing mark*

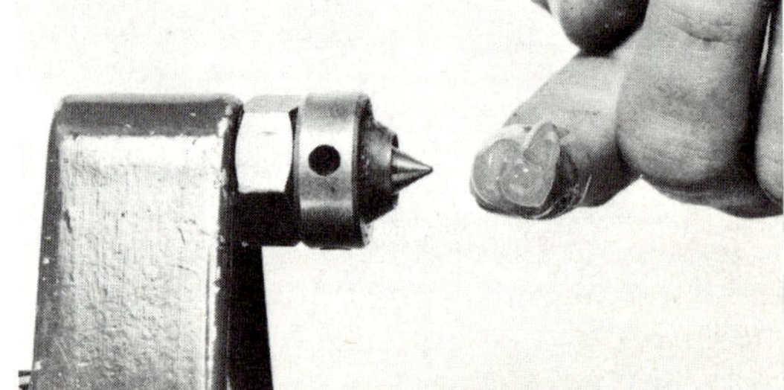

*To reduce friction, grease 'dog' before securing the work in the lathe*

sharpened at an angle or straight across.

Long and strong chisels, which are made in the same sizes as the standard chisels, have stronger, thicker blades.

Gouges are of two types: standard, made in sizes of 6mm–25mm, and long, made in sizes of 10mm, 13mm, 19mm and 25mm. The latter type has a much stronger blade and is suitable for heavier work.

Gouges are used for roughing — that is turning the work roughly to size. If you are turning between centres a 25mm gouge with the cutting edge ground squarely across is best.

When turning a box or bowl the gouge corners should be ground well back to prevent the edges digging in and scarring the wood. These corners are automatically taken off if the correct bevel is ground on the gouge.

The parting tool, designed for parting off, or separating the end waste, is in one size only.

*Scraping tools*
Scraping tools are often classified as chisels. The round-nose and diamond-point tools are made in 13mm, 19mm and 25mm sizes.

## Tool handles

Wood-turning tool handles are made of beech with strong brass ferrules. They are longer than ordinary tool handles, bulbous in shape, with a small diameter end.

The shaping gives correct hand holding, even for small hands, and sufficient leverage to counteract the revolving timber.

## Callipers

Callipers are used to check turned work for correct final inside and outside sizes. There are two types of calliper: tight-joint and screw.

To adjust tight-joint callipers tap the arms further apart or closer together as necessary.

Screw, or adjustable, callipers, with slip cone nuts, are more expensive, but they can be quickly reset by the adjusting screw.

## Templates

Templates can be made from cardboard, plywood or hardboard, or a metal-spiked tool such as the Copydex Mimic. They are cut to the contours of the work to be turned. A template is useful when repetition-cutting.

Templates may be half- or full-length. Mark the diameter of the work at each end of the template. Turn these to size, first

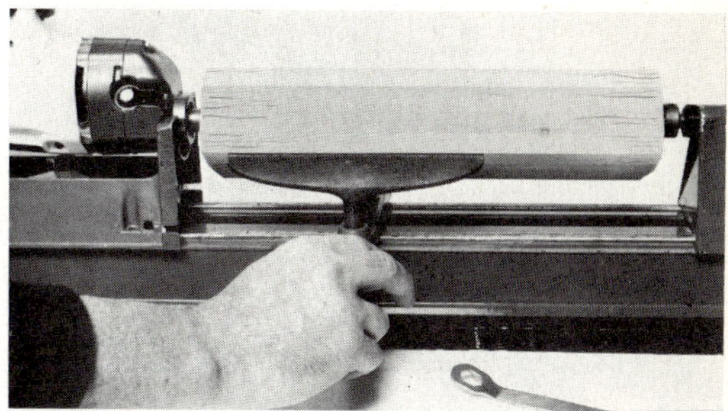

*Set rest 3mm below centre and from work*

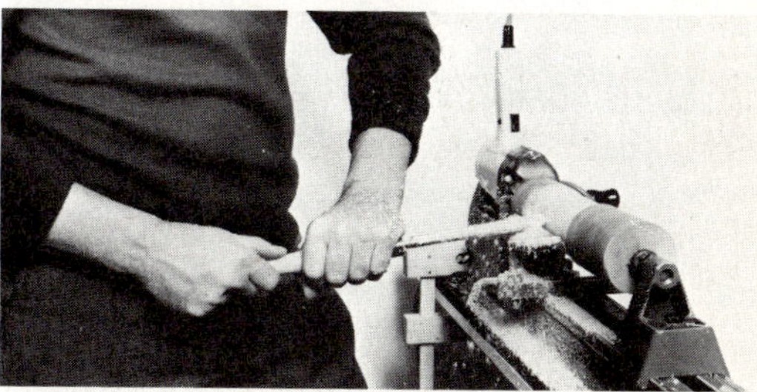

*Use slow speed for rough turning*

*Using profile former to check work*

*For final finishing, use fine glass or garnet paper to smooth*

on the timber. Use the template to check the work at frequent intervals.

## Grinding and sharpening

Good results are impossible if you do not see that the tools are sharp and correctly shaped before starting work.

All tools are ground but must be sharpened or 'whetted' before use. Sharpen using an India stone or medium grit.

Before using the stone, smear a few drops of light machine oil or neatsfoot on the surface. After use, wipe the stone clean.

Gouges are ground at 30° and sharpened on the ground face, as they have no sharpening bevel. The bevel must follow the curve of the tool.

When using a flat oilstone, hone the gouge by holding it in one hand and then rub the hand-held stone flat against the bevel. The gouge should be rotated against the stone during sharpening. The bevel must be kept flat; careless use of the oilstone very quickly produces a rounded stone.

Once a wire edge appears on the inside, concave, side of the gouge, extending along the whole edge, take this off by using an oilstone 'slip' held flat in the groove of the gouge. Make a few strokes with the round edge.

The turning chisel is often supplied with a curved side elevation; this should be ground flat for it to cut effectively. It is sharpened in much the same way as an ordinary woodworking chisel. Regrinding or coarse honing must preserve the original curve.

Both bevels on a chisel should be ground at between 20° and 30° to the side; they are sharpened only on the ground face. Scraping chisels are ground at between 30° and 45° on one side only and sharpened on this face.

Longer bevels will cause 'chattering' in use, with deterioration of the edge. Parting tools are sharpened in the same way as chisels.

Wood can be shaped in two ways — by scraping or by peeling with woodcutting tools. The latter needs a thin, sharp blade held almost flat to the surface.

The thickness of the shaving can be adjusted by slight changes in the blade angle, while you steady the blade by pressing the flat against the surface to ensure fairly effortless cutting.

In scraping, drag the sharp edge over the surface at right angles but just below the centre. Initially it is easier to work using the scraping rather than the peeling method.

Hold the tool firmly on to the rest with the left hand, while keeping the handle against the hip with the right. This also helps to deflect shavings away from the body.

The tool tip should touch the work just above an imaginary centre line between the head and tail dogs.

A good cut can be taken but the final surface will have a ribbed appearance.

This can be improved by using a round-nosed gouge turned on to its side so that it cuts with a chisel action.

To produce a planed surface, use either a skew chisel or a chisel ground squarely across and bevelled on both sides.

This is laid flat on the rest with the chisel resting on the work. As the right hand is raised, the chisel will begin to cut the wood quite close to the top edge. Use only the lower part of the chisel edge, turning the tool over when moving in the opposite direction.

Whether working with a gouge or a chisel, always keep the bevel in contact with the timber, as this will prevent the edge from digging in.

Care must be taken to ensure that the point of the chisel is always clear of the work. The thickness of shavings is controlled by the lift given to the tool by the right hand.

When using a cutting tool, cut from right to left when using the left corner of the gouge, and from left to right with the gouge's right corner.

Once the work is roughly turned, increase the speed and use the chisels to clean up.

Turn the work down to its maximum overall diameter, working along the entire length of the tool rest. Move the rest progressively towards the tailstock until the piece is entirely round.

Work from left to right, or if left-handed from right to left. Use timber slightly over the maximum dimensions needed, for wood can be turned down very quickly, and you may easily find yourself with a piece that is undersized. Always advance the tool carefully to the work to gauge the amount of cut.

Scraping chisels may be used when working between centres but the tool rest must be dropped slightly below centre and the chisel held flat on the rest.

Keep the tool rest as close as possible to the work and advance the tool carefully to the work, to gauge the amount of cut accurately.

Control the cutting edge of the tool by moving it in an arc — up and down to control the depth of cut, and to each side for width.

To make a long cut parallel with the rest, build this up in a series of shallow curves. These will appear initially wavy, but will finish flat if you make one light continuous

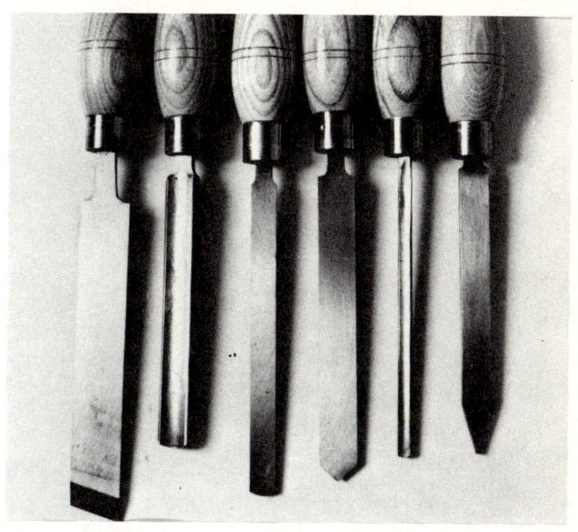

*A basic set of wood-turning tools includes various gouges and chisels*

final cut. Do not slide the tool along the rest to make the cut.

If you keep the tool edge really sharp, carefully removing only a little waste at a time, you will have little to do by way of final finishing with glass or garnet paper.

Once you have turned the piece of work, use the parting chisel to separate it from the waste ends, which carry the indentations of the steel dogs.

This is presented to the work at right angles with the bevel rubbing the work.

The thickness of cut can be controlled by raising the right hand.

Do not cut entirely through the wood but only to a depth of 25mm all round, then remove the piece from the lathe and finish off with a tenon saw.

## Face-plate turning

For most face-plate work — that is over about 40mm in diameter — you should work at the lower speed on a two-speed drill.

Partially prepare timber by taking off any initial corners, by first marking diagonals to find the centre and then taking off radial lines so that you can accurately cut off the surplus corner material.

When using the face-plate to turn the inside of a bowl or lampshade base, first drill a series of holes in the base of the roughly shaped object, using the vertical drill stand, so that you then have substantially less waste to remove on the lathe.

Wood-turning tools will stay sharper in this way and you will find it a lot quicker and easier to do the job.

Position the face-plate on your prepared blank, facing downwards, and fix it in position with four short screws through the back of the plate.

Use a bradawl to mark the screw positions. Screw the face-plate into the drill spindle and set the tool rest so that it just clears the corners of the blank. Check this by turning the face-plate by hand.

Work first on the edges to even out the corners, using the scraping tool. Tools should be firmly but comfortably held and presented to the work at the correct angle.

When bowl-turning, the gouge must have the shoulders ground well back and set against the wood so that the bevel rubs against the work.

The round-nose scraper is a useful tool here, but it must be held flat on the rest, which should be slightly below centre. Keep the rest as close to the revolving work as possible.

Never lean over work on the lathe, for example when you want to work on the inside hollow of a bowl.

So that the screw holes do not show in the base of the finished piece, you can fix a piece of scrap to the attachment with the chuck screw, and sandwich a piece of thin card of brown paper between.

When finished, you can simply slice through this sandwich to remove the object, then smooth the bottom to remove the remains of the paper and adhesive.

Whether turning between centres or on the face-plate, sharp tools achieve a surface that only needs rubbing with fine glass-paper and polish to finish off.

Take the tool rest out of the way, as this can be dangerous. Hold the glasspaper at each end with your fingers, clear of the revolving surface and at the back of the work, and move the paper across the back of the work.

A quick finish for natural wood can be achieved by pressing a piece of beeswax, carnauba wax or, less preferably, candle wax against the spinning wood; the wax will melt by friction and flow over the surface. Then, hold a pad of cloth against the surface to remove surplus wax, and polish the wood at the same time. The rule is: put a little on but take a lot off.

# Rotary tools and flexible drive

Rotary tools include rasps, routers, files and profiling cutters which can fit into the power drill chuck or be used with the flexible drive, the latter giving greater control of cutting angles.

Rasps are used largely for roughing out and shaping wood, plastics and laminates and are made with a choice of conical, cylindrical and spherical heads.

The drill can be mounted in a horizontal or vertical drill stand, leaving both hands free to control the work.

Profile cutting is simpler if the drill is mounted in a vertical stand. This allows you to adjust the height of the drill carriage to permit the tool to engage the work at the correct depth.

Rasps should be used at the fastest drill speed, while rotary tools used on metal should run at a slow speed.

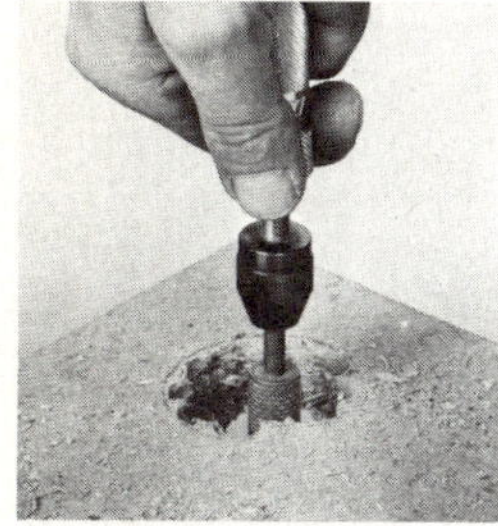

*Rasp fitted in flexible drive used to enlarge a hole in timber*

*Hole can then be finished off neatly*

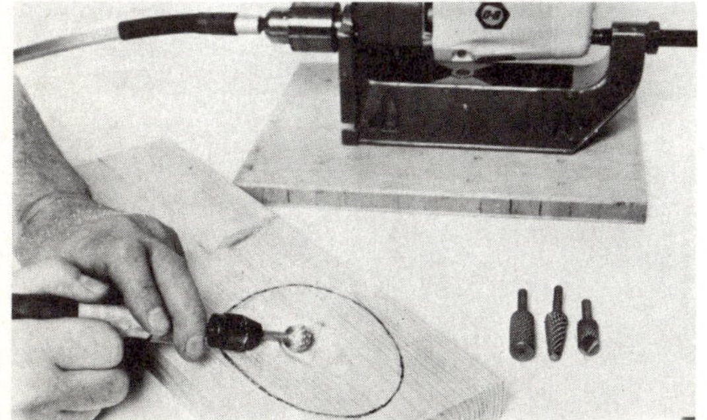

*Attachment can be used with rasp to make a shallow dish or an ashtray*

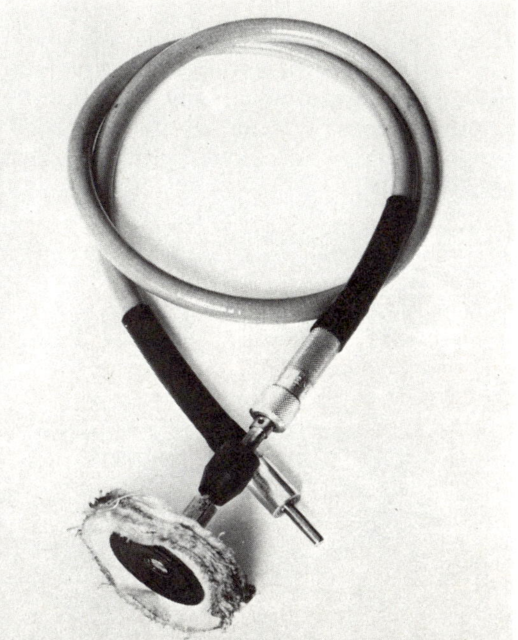

*Flexible drive fits into drill chuck and can accept range of attachments*

*Rag buff is one of the attachments which gives control for polishing work*

# Spray painters

With an electrically operated hand spray gun you can achieve a professional painting finish, as well as spraying other liquids. Only a fine spray of paint is applied to the area, and it dries before any dust can settle and mar the surface. It is also a quick way of spreading an even paint surface. You can use a spray gun in or out of doors.

The most versatile form of hand spray gun works on an airless principle. The gun is operated with a self-contained airless pump. This type of pump reduces bounce and over-spray to a minimum. Spray guns should work at a pressure of at least $28kg/cm^2$.

A compressor enables a wider range of spray jobs to be tackled, though the techniques of use are similar.

An airless spray gun consists of a pump and mechanism housed within a plastic body. The body of the Black & Decker airless spray gun has a pistol grip to hold the unit and is operated by a trigger on the handle.

An airless spray gun atomizes sprayable liquids. The electromagnetic mechanism drives a pump which delivers paint under vacuum and high pressures through the jet. This achieves spraying with less mist and wastage.

Like other power tools, the paint spray gun connects through a cable to a suitable mains outlet point.

Paint is poured into a 800cc capacity plastic container, which screws to the base of the spray unit. As this is transparent, it is easy to see at a glance how much paint you have in the container.

Various nozzles can be fitted, and you can also make different settings, so that you can control and deliver only the quantity of paint necessary. You may need to apply several coats to cover the surface satisfactorily.

The paint used must be clean and of the correct viscosity: high-viscosity paints are best for *brush* painting; spray paints must be diluted to be of the correct, lower, viscosity. Paint manufacturers sometimes indicate on the labels of paint tins the necessary degree of thinning needed.

Dirt and foreign material in the paint may clog the jets and the pump, so all paint should first be filtered. If you do not have a filter, a nylon stocking is quite satisfactory.

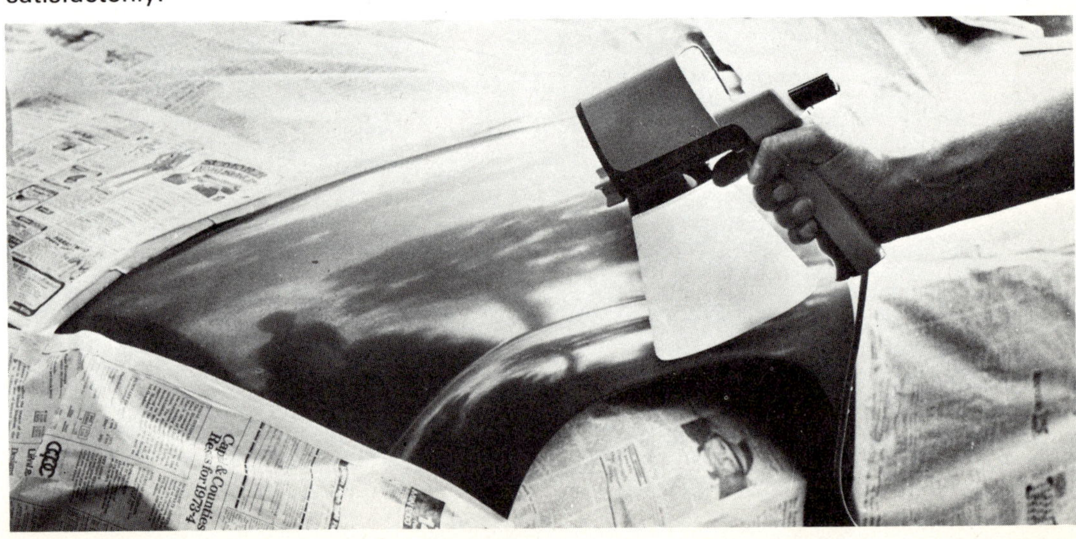

## Thinning Chart

| Type | Thinning required | Number of coats | Remarks |
|---|---|---|---|
| *Gloss paints | 2–4 parts paint<br>1–3 parts thinner | 3 light coats | 10 minutes between coats 1 and 2;<br>20 minutes between coats 2 and 3 |
| Gloss paints | 2–3 parts paint<br>1 part thinner | 2 or 3 light coats | 20 minutes between coats |
| Emulsion (for absorbent surfaces, e.g. walls/ceilings) | 1–2 parts paint<br>1–1½ parts water | 3 light coats | 20 minutes between coats |
| Water paints | 1–2 parts paint<br>1–3 parts water | 2 light coats | 15 minutes between coats |
| Cellulose (paint and primer) | 1 part paint<br>1 part thinner | As required | 20 minutes between coats (ensure ventilation) |
| Creosote/wood dye | None | As required | |
| French polish | 2 parts polish<br>1 part thinner | As required | 20 minutes between coats |
| Insecticides | As specified by manufacturer | As required | Do not spray into the wind |

* Quick-drying gloss paints are suggested

Almost any type of paint is suitable for spray application. Using the correct thinner for the product, wood preservative, water-based, oil-based, polyurethane and bituminous paint can all be sprayed. Water- or oil-based paint is normally thinned by a third to a half, while other paints, such as lacquer, may need equal parts of paint to thinner.

Viscosities are graded in seconds. A viscosity measuring cup, available as an extra, helps to establish the right viscosity by measuring the speed, in seconds, at which a given measure of paint in the cup empties. The cup gives viscosities of up to 35 seconds.

When liquids are used containing materials such as chalk, lime, red lead or acids, the pump mechanism and the jet are subject to a higher degree of wear.

The Black & Decker pump is controlled by a knob on the back of the spray body. Turning this counter-clockwise gives a wide spray cone with a high delivery of paint. Turned clockwise, a smaller spraying cone, and a lower volume of paint is delivered.

## Masking

Before starting work ensure that all areas that are not to be painted are masked. Special care should be taken to mask window and door areas. This can be done with newspaper and masking tape. Tape with a low-impact adhesive is most useful as it is quite easily peeled off once the paint has dried. Leave the masking tape in place until the paint has dried thoroughly.

## Interior decorating

When decorating indoors aim to clear the area completely. If this is not possible, stack all the furniture in the middle of the room and cover it with dust or polythene sheets.

To prevent seepage of atomized paint, which gets everywhere, the polythene sheeting may be stapled to bare floor-boards. Good ventilation is essential when using a spray gun.

Never smoke when working with a spray gun or use it near a naked flame; remember the pilot lights of gas appliances — these should be turned off.

## External decorating

When spraying the outside walls of a building it is not necessary to mask the rainwater goods or woodwork if these are due to be painted. However, decorative paths, patios or driveways must be covered as they may be very difficult to clean later. You may have to experiment to find the right consistency that allows the paint to atomize as it is ejected from the nozzle. A clogged nozzle can usually be freed with a thin piece of wire.

Primer coats should be applied with a brush. This 'teases' the paint to produce a better bond. Sprayed paint tends to 'lie' on the surface.

## Accessories

For most home-decorating jobs only two basic nozzles are needed. These are the plain, round nozzle and the fish-tail or fan-shaped nozzle. There is also a flexible extension nozzle which is useful for less accessible places such as ceilings.

Always keep a spray gun upright during use. If it is inadvertently turned upside down it will cease to work.

## Spraying

Before using the gun, spray some thinners to make sure that the mechanism is clear.

Prepare and prime the surface to be painted. Test the spray application on a piece of hardboard or any waste surface. This will enable you to check the paint consistency and paint-covering capacity.

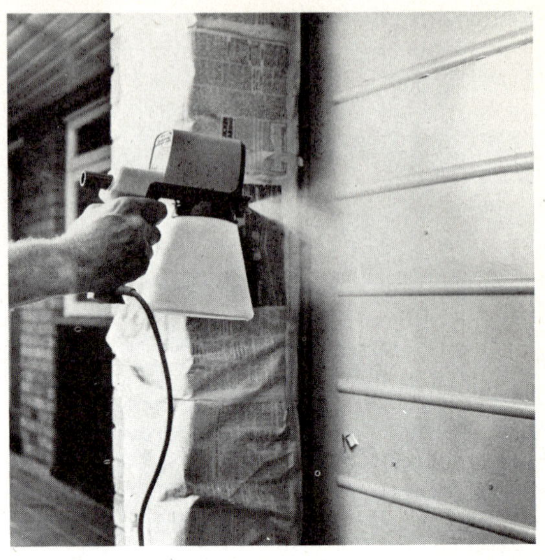

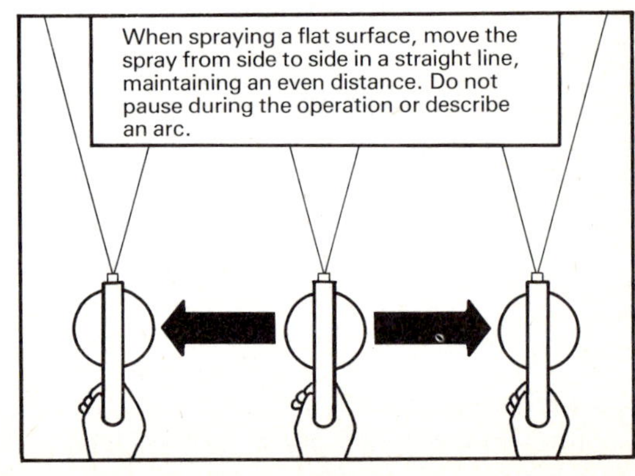

Ideally, the work should be carried out in clean, dry, relatively warm, still conditions – temperature around 21 °C. If the temperature is lower, the surface will take longer to dry. Wind will carry the spray, plus airborne dust and insects, which will mar the finished paint surface.

A spraying distance depending on viscosity, but in general of between 250mm and 300mm, should be chosen for maximum delivery of paint, reduced to between 100mm and 200mm for the finer setting, in which case the gun should also be moved slightly more quickly.

Keep the gun in a horizontal position with the jet nozzle pointing slightly downwards. The distance between the object being sprayed and the gun should remain constant. The nozzle should be at right angles to the surface. This is most easily achieved if the gun is moved with the full length of the arm and not from the wrist.

Operate the spray just slightly before you reach the edge of the surface you are spraying. Larger areas are best sprayed in a criss-cross fashion, by starting first horizontally from left to right, slightly lower down from right to left, and then vertically from top to bottom and a little further over from bottom to top.

Do not use an arcing motion, as this will cause paint to be deposited unevenly. Use wide horizontal strokes and a continuous, steady action. Even a momentary stop will cause the paint to run at that spot. Release the trigger at the end of each stroke. This prevents heavy over-spray.

To obtain an even coverage overlap slightly at the end of each stroke. Allow the paint to dry thoroughly before applying the second and third coats. This will not cause any problem or hinder work as application and drying are quick.

If the paint is not allowed to dry thoroughly it may 'curtain', or run, or a pimply orange-peel effect may occur. Gloss paint must not be applied too thickly or it will run and look unsightly.

To minimize the dripping of paint on vertical areas, it is best to apply a light coat with the gun positioned further away from the object and then to finish spraying at the specified distance.

Horizontal surfaces are best started at one end, striking the surface with the spray at an angle of about 45°. The over-spray is covered by the following stroke in the next upwards application.

With a little practice, a very even surface can be achieved with a spray gun. This is essential on interior surfaces. Externally, when using a spray gun to decorate rendered walls, the elimination of runs or unevenness is not so important.

Always make sure that the paint container and mechanism are cleaned thoroughly after use. Water can be used to clean the unit after using water-based paints; thinners or white spirit must be used for other types of paint. Remove the spray heads, clean and dry these separately.

After cleaning, spray some light mineral oil on the metal surfaces to prevent corrosion of the mechanism. Cleaning should be started immediately after you finish painting, so that the paint does not have time to dry.

If the mechanism is not cleaned thoroughly and becomes clogged, you will hear a low humming noise when you press the trigger but the unit will not work. Then it will be necessary to strip down the pump and clean it with thinners.

This is done in the following way. First, remove the nozzle by turning it counter-clockwise. Then remove the valve and place both parts in thinners. Unscrew the cover of the unit by removing the screw on the upper back part of the unit and two screws on the back of the handle, and remove the volume control by turning it counter-clockwise.

Take out its control spring. Lift the leaf-spring with a screwdriver, pull back the spring armature and remove it by lifting upwards.

Place the unit on its back so that the front cylinder opening is pointing upwards. Pour some thinners into the bore of the cylinder and allow it to soak for a few minutes.

Place a 2—3mm diameter dowel on top of the pistol and give it a slight tap with a hammer to move the piston towards the rear, so that the piston and spring can be pulled out of the cylinder.

Assembly is carried out in the reverse order. The piston with its spring is assembled from the back. Place the swing armature on the piston plate and connect the leaf spring to the drive.

An additional paint container (with a cover) allows you to have separate paints ready if necessary, so that you can speed up work.

The standard diameter nozzle supplied is 0·5mm, and this is suitable for general uses. Other nozzles available as extras are 0·4mm nozzle for very fine atomization of liquids of very low viscosity — thinners, water, thin oils; a 0·8mm nozzle for liquids of high viscosity, where the finish is of secondary importance, and for medium high-viscosity liquids; a 1·0mm nozzle for high-viscosity mediums. The spray nozzle extension is flexible and used for spraying into awkward shapes or difficult spots, such as the backs of radiators.

A needle-jet extension accessory produces a concentrated jet without atomization and is used for jobs such as cleaning motors, spraying oil on springs and spraying timber-preservation fluids. But it cannot be used to spray paints or lacquers.

An injection extension is used for moth-proofing upholstery. This cannot be used with paints.

## Compressor

Another form of the spray unit is the compressor, which is able to produce highly professional spray work and can also do other jobs, such as inflating tyres, foot-balls, rubber dinghies and balloons and, with a caulking attachment, filling cracks, pointing walls and applying adhesives. There are also a garden spray nozzle,

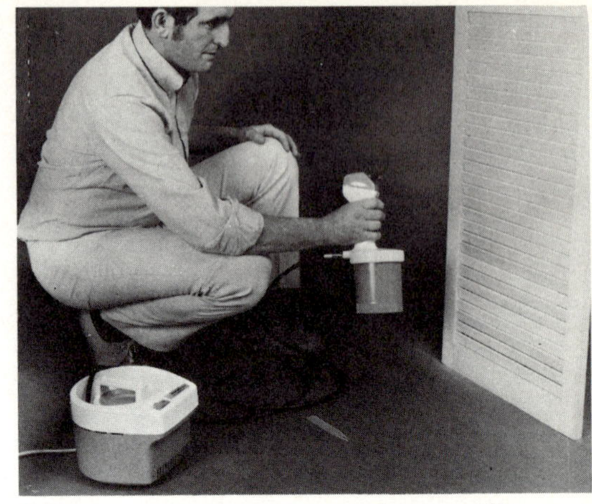

*Linear-motor compressor is versatile*

extension hoses, filters and paint strainers, and a face mask.

The compressor is the first domestic application of the linear motor, which has been applied to the prototype hovertrain. The motor has only three moving parts — piston, valve and spring. An electromagnet draws the piston back until the current is interrupted and a spring returns the piston to its original position.

The motor has been miniaturized in the double-insulated compressor, which has all the qualities of the conventional diaphragm and piston-type compressor but none of their disadvantages.

The unit produces oil-free air up to 41–42kgf/m² — some 1·40kgf/m² (kilograms/force per square metre) more than equivalent diaphragm models. It operates at constant pressure without fluctuation or pulsation during spraying.

The gun is of the bleeder type which gives a constant flow, making it possible to spray all types of paint, latex, varnishes, liquid garden chemicals and insecticides. It has a full 750cc capacity cylinder and standard and trimmer nozzles.

The compressor weighs only 3·90kg and is supplied with spray gun, inflator kit and viscosity guide, plus some 2·44m of hose and 1·83m of cable.

## Paint mixer

This tool can take a great deal of hard work out of stirring paint — and it can do it more thoroughly than by hand, because you can get right to the bottom of the tin with the stirrer.

If not used correctly, however, a large amount of paint will be quickly distributed in a wide circle around the paint tin.

The attachment consists of a curved or angled metal bar which fits into the drill chuck. The drill is operated at the fast speed.

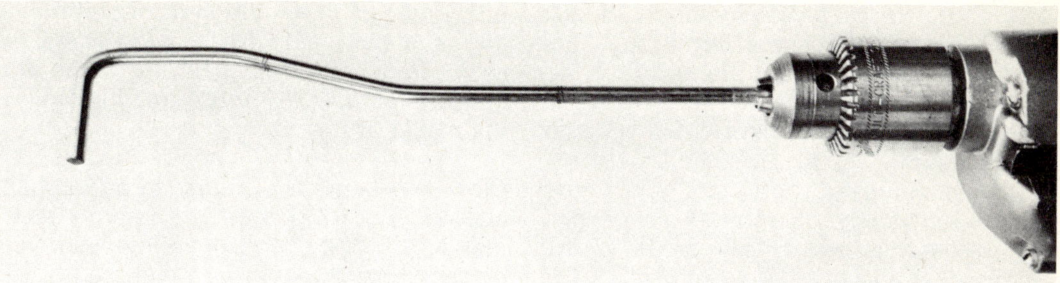

*Paint stirrer — an angled rod — fits into the chuck of a power drill*

Stand the tin on a firm base, covered with a polythene sheet or sheet of newspaper, so that you can work over it without being at an awkward angle and risking upsetting the paint. A large tin is easier to hold between your feet.

Place the attachment into the paint to the *bottom* of the tin *before* switching on. After switching off, allow the motor to stop before you withdraw it.

To clean the mixer, remove it from the drill chuck and wash under the tap (for water-based paints) or insert into a shallow depth of solvent in a deep container, withdrawing it slowly while it is still running. Avoid highly volatile solvents whose vapour could be ignited by the sparking of the motor.

*Insert the stirrer fully into the paint. Ensure that drill stops before removing*

# Power vacuum cleaner

One of the more tedious aspects of any do-it-yourself job, in the home or in the workshop, is clearing up the mess.

A heavy-duty, all-purpose electric vacuum cleaner such as the Black & Decker Majorvac can make short work of cleaning up a wide variety of debris from plaster, wood shavings and broken glass to the normal dust and household dirt.

Unlike the conventional vacuum cleaner, which should never be used to pick up highly volatile materials such as sawdust, the Majorvac has an enclosed motor which is shielded from sparks, and is thus perfectly safe to use in a workshop.

The Majorvac weighs 6·60kg and is easily transported. It has a suitcase-type handle and a four-wheeled trolley for easy manoeuvrability. Powered by a 850W motor, the machine sucks up debris through a wide-bore, 63mm diameter inlet hose into a 19-litre capacity steel drum, the top of which unclips for easy emptying.

An adaptor converts the hose for 30mm attachments, providing increased suction, which makes the machine an efficient household vacuum cleaner. The cleaner is supplied with a cable drum to store 5·50m of cable.

A choice of nine different attachments makes it adaptable for a wide range of uses, from cleaning carpets, rugs and upholstery, to walls, floors and shelving or the inside of the car.

Cloth and paper filter bags, an attachment adaptor, the trolley and two 30mm attachments, a crevice tool, a 150mm general-purpose head, four 63mm attachments, two 500mm rigid extensions, a 150mm rect-angular hose nozzle with a brush and a

1·52m flexible hose are supplied as standard with the machine.

Extra accessories, 30mm attachments, include a 150m brush shoe, a round brush, a 250mm master head, brush shoe, rug shampoo attachments and an extension hose extending to about 1·83m.

Extra 63mm attachments are a 350mm floor nozzle with a brush and a crevice tool.

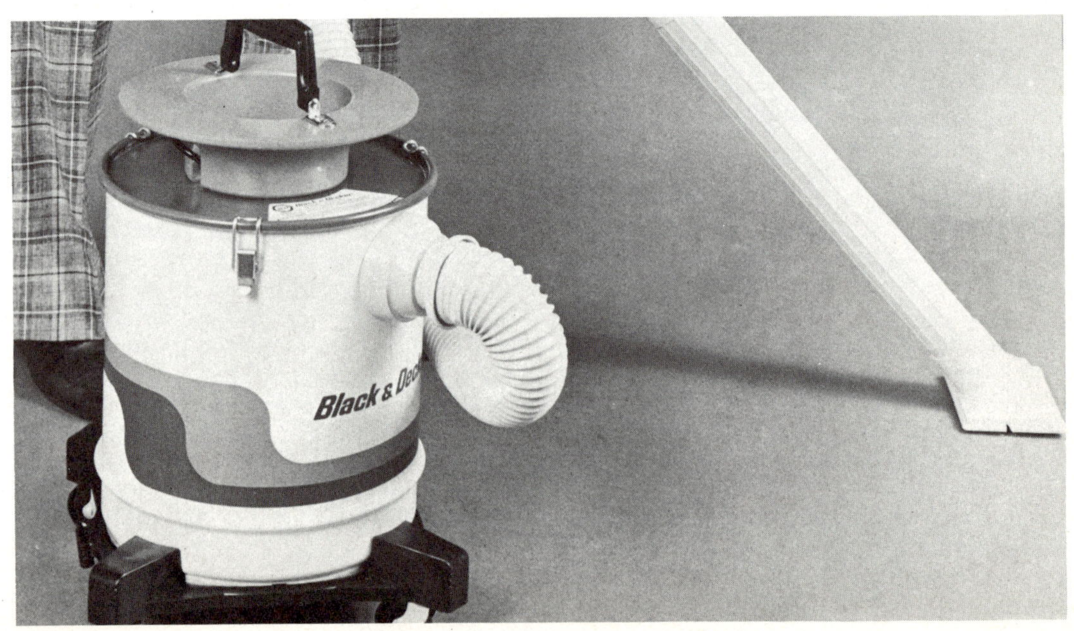

# Power tools in the garden

Power tools, such as lawnmowers, lawn edge trimmers, shears, cordless and integral trimmers and hedge-trimmer attachments, can cut out much of the hard work and tedious monotony that is involved in keeping even the smallest garden area neat and trim throughout the summer months.

There are three main garden power tools that make gardening easier and more enjoyable: rotary and cylinder lawnmowers, and hedge trimmers.

## Cylinder mowers

The tough power-driven cylinder mower, with 305mm or 355mm width blades, is a robust yet light-weight garden tool, which reduces much of the effort in mowing.

There are three models in the Black & Decker cylinder mower Lawnrazor range. The machines are plugged into a cable to the mains and operated by a handle switch.

The blades are powered, but the machine has to be pushed. The 7800 cuts per minute blade action makes lawn cutting a fast, easy job. The cutting height of the blades is adjustable.

Each model can be fitted with a tough non-rust polypropylene grass box and is heavy enough to give the attractive striped effect that finishes off the appearance of a newly cut lawn.

All models have self-adjusting handles and a safety on—off switch. The 305mm models are supplied with 15m of two-core cable, the 355mm model with 25m. Connection to all machines, which are double-insulated, is by a two-pin plug.

It is important to keep the cable well out of the way of blades during mowing. A cable-control guide, suitable for all the cylinder mowers, attaches to the central cross-bar

*Lawnrazor cylinder mower makes 7800 cuts a minute; keep cable clear*

of the mower handle to ensure the cable is kept clear of the mower when in operation.

Another useful accessory is a cable-securing strap, which prevents cable connections coming apart.

Always remember that the blades continue to rotate for a few seconds after the motor is switched off, so do not immediately put your hands near the blades. The mower should be disconnected from the mains supply before making any adjustment.

The machine has a life-sealed gear box that needs no lubrication. Replacement blades are available for all models of cylinder mowers.

## Rotary mowers

The electric rotary motor, with models weighing between about 4·55kg and 5·55kg, combines lightness and effective rotary cutting action with a reliable power source.

The rotary principle utilizes a fan-type blade, driven by a motor in which the action of the rotor strikes the grass at speed to cut it. It is possible to cut long, wet grass or even to hit stones without causing trouble.

The machine is very simple. It consists of a tempered steel cutter fixed centrally to the end of an electric power unit. The motor

*Lawnderette rotary mower is double-insulated with safety cut-out switch*

*The unit has choice of three blade heights to suit mowing conditions*

is enclosed in a steel cowl for safety. This covers the cutter, the whole assembly riding on a split roller at the back and two front wheels. There are less expensive models which have two sets of wheels.

### Adjusting the setting

During the growing season the lawn should be cut with the blade of the mower set at different heights, depending on the length of grass. Adjustment of the cutting heights is simple.

Release the wheels by slacking off the spindle nuts so you can adjust to either the low, medium or high position provided by the shaped slots in the housing. Once the wheels are set in the required position, retighten the spindle nuts.

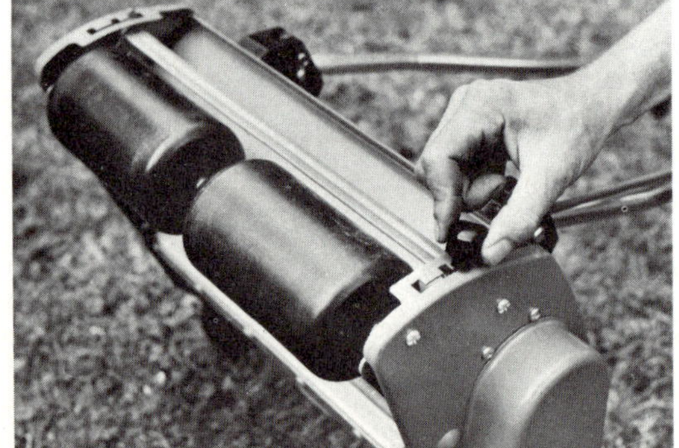

*The Lawnrazor light-weight mower also has a height-of-cut adjustment*

Depending on the type of grass, the height of the cutter should be adjusted during the cutting season. During March to the middle of April set it to high (25–30mm) and keep it at medium (25mm) from the middle of April to the end of May.

During June and July have the blade at the lowest setting (75–100mm). Up to the middle of September take it back to the medium setting, then set it at high until the end of October. By varying the settings, growth of the rough grasses will be discouraged.

An electric rotary mower can be used in conjunction with a larger motor mower to cut extensive areas of grass. Cut the main area of the lawn with the heavier mower, leaving a strip between 150mm and 350mm wide round the edge.

This edge can then be cut more easily with the lighter machine, which will not, if used properly, crush the edges of the lawn.

A lighter, more easily handled, machine is useful for negotiating steep banks, narrow paths and anywhere it is not possible to use a bigger machine.

Cutting round grass verges can be done with a rotary mower. Allow the cutter to overhang one edge but press down the handle to keep the weight of the mower on the rear roller or wheels. This prevents the cutter from tilting over and gouging into the soil.

A rotary mower is controlled by an on—off trigger mounted in the moulded pistol-grip handle. This switch has a locking button. When switched on, the motor is kept running and is released only by a second depression of the switch.

An overload device, an automatic thermal switch, is housed in the moulded handle to switch off if the motor overloads.

If the motor shows signs of distress through overloading, switch off immediately the cut-out operates. Once the cause of overloading has been removed, press the cut-out button to reset the device and then restart the motor by pressing the switch trigger.

### Double insulation
Motor mowers are double-insulated and require no earthing. Connection to the mains is through the hand-grip switch and a short length of two- or three-core cable terminating in a two- or three-pin connector.

The socket end of the connector fits to the end of the mains lead. In the two-core lead only the live and neutral conductors are connected to the two-pin connector.

Usually, the garden power tool is supplied with a short length of lead and a connector. You can obtain the extension cable separately, choosing a length suitable for your needs. More cable than you need is merely difficult to handle and store.

The mains cable should stretch easily from the nearest power point to the furthest area to be cut. Allow for, in the length, fixed obstacles such as greenhouses, sheds or pools that may have to be negotiated, taking up more cable than the mean length required.

Lengths of up to 60m can be used with a power mower; much over this, the resistance factor may prevent the motor reaching full capacity, and a cable specially designed for use over a specified distance may have to be used.

Cable is most easily stored on a portable reel, from which it can be unrolled. It can be stored neatly and tangle-free.

### Using the cable
As the cable reel cannot be rotated once the extension cable is plugged into the mains socket, unroll the amount needed along the garden. Provided you work to a regular pattern, you can cut grass without the hazard of catching the cable in the blade.

### Mowing the lawn
A striped pattern is popular with many gardeners and gives a neat, well-manicured look to the lawn. It is achieved, whether using a cylinder or rotary mower, in the following way. (This method ensures that the cable is under control and not accidentally cut during mowing.)

Use the right hand to guide the mower, the left to control the cable. Allow about 1m of slack cable between your hand and the connector. As you work along the first strip of lawn, pull off the slack as necessary.

Make a right-hand turn at the top of the strip, jerking the cable so that a loop is formed beyond the turning point; allow enough slack to pass behind you when you change direction.

Move across the lawn away from the parked cable reel working up and down the lawn, slightly overlapping the previously cut strip with the next cut.

Always turn away from the cable between finishing one strip and starting back the other way. Once you finish, at the far side of the lawn, switch off at the mains, disconnect the cable from the mower and wind it back on to the reel.

A rotary electric mower can cope with long, wet grass, but it may, to avoid overloading the motor, have to be a two-stage operation.

Overloading may occur when long stems of grass wind round the cutter, become wedged against the cover and act as an effectual brake to the machine.

This can be avoided by setting the cutter as high as possible, lowering the handle to tilt up the front end of the mower and working forward a little way into the grass. As you work, slowly raise the handle until the front wheels are resting on the ground.

Next, lower the handle and cut the next piece of long grass. Rake off the cut grass as you work. This makes the job easier and cuts down the risk of long grass becoming entwined round the cutter and putting the machine under stress.

If the motor does slow down, indicating that it is working under stress, switch off, disconnect at the mains and clean out the inside of the cover.

*Old lawns*
An old, uneven or neglected lawn may need preliminary treatment before cutting. Dead grass and leaves should be removed with a grass rake before the lawn is cut. This makes the job easier and prevents the risk of overloading the motor.

For an uneven lawn, first use the machine with the cutters set in the highest position. Then roll the lawn, with a heavy roller, before giving a closer mowing.

The rotating blades of the mower throw the grass cuttings to the right. When cutting small areas, keep the machine moving to the left which will prevent it from becoming clogged with the grass you have just cut.

A rotary mower does not have a box to collect the lawn cuttings, working on the principle that power lawn mowing is quick, can be done more frequently than conventional mowing, and that the cuttings produced are so fine that they soon wither away.

**Edging tools**
Edging tools, whether battery or mains-operated, apart from taking some of the hard work off your shoulders, are complementary in use with the power lawnmower and are able to deal with awkward corners, edgings near pools and rockeries and so on.

These jobs are tedious and time-consuming, yet properly done they give the final finished look to the cared-for garden.

*Cordless grass shears*
The cordless grass shear makes lawn edge trimming a quick and easy job. Run on nickel-cadmium batteries, which are recharged with a supplied charger, the grass shear will cut up to 205m$^2$ of area without recharging. It can also be used to trim back light hedge or shrub growth.

The light-weight, hand-held unit has a switch-locking button and trigger incorporated into the handle. The business end consists of two cutting blades, the lower stationary, the upper a moving blade, made of high-quality, heat-treated steel which holds a sharp edge over a long period.

*Cordless grass shears can be used for grass, shrubs or in awkward corners*

The shear is always immediately ready to run. To prevent accidents a safety switch-locking button is incorporated in the handle. Before attempting to turn the switch on, disconnect the shear from the charger. The switch-locking button should be in the lock position.

To switch on, turn the lock-on button to the left or right, slide the locking button back with your thumb, hold it momentarily and squeeze the trigger switch. Once you have finished using the tool, release the trigger. The locking switch will then snap on, preventing the trigger from being pressed accidentally.

Always ensure the lock-on switch is in the 'on' position when leaving the tool unattended.

The shear can be used to trim round awkward and inaccessible parts of the garden — under trees, round flower beds, under fences and along walls. It can also cope with light growth on shrubs or hedges.

If the blades jam, turn the tool off and use a short piece of stick to remove the obstruction. While the shear will normally run for thirty to forty minutes without recharging, heavy growth or dirty, blunt blades will shorten the effective cutting time.

A blade sharpener, standard with the 8282 shear and an accessory with the 8280, is useful for sharpening the blades and provides a good protective sheath for the blades when not in use.

*Sharpening*
To maintain maximum efficiency the moving blade should be sharpened frequently and certainly after three trimming jobs.

Place the sharpener on a flat surface. Tilt the shear forward, placing the two outer ends of the stationary blade into the two recesses in the front of the sharpener. Next, lower the shear until the back of the blade snaps down on to the back of the sharpener.

Turn the tool on for about a minute. Turn off and test the blades for sharpness. If the shear is not cutting cleanly repeat the procedure.

*Cleaning*
Blades must be kept clean if cutting efficiency is to be maintained. A quick check for dirt or sap on the blades is to switch off: if the blades stop almost immediately, they need cleaning.

This is simply done by applying a liquid ammonia-based cleaner at full strength to the blades. Allow this to soak in and then use a stiff brush to loosen the dirt.

Either immerse the blades — not the motor — in a bowl of hot water or hold under a tap. Turn the tool on for about ten seconds. Turn off and wipe the blades dry with a clean cloth.

Remember, blades are sharp. As the shear runs on a low-voltage supply there is no danger of an electric shock, but take care to keep the motor out of the water. Once dry the blades can be lubricated with a dry spray lubricant.

*Safety*
Safety is as important when using the cordless garden shear as with any other power tool. It is preferable to trim grass on a dry day — although damp grass will not give an electric shock. Always check, before cutting, for obstacles such as lighting cables or large stones. If you hit a stone you may dent a blade. If this happens and interferes with cutting, use a fine-toothed file or sharpening stone to remove the nick.

Always keep your hands well away from the moving blades. Feed the blade into the grass steadily: do not force it. If the blades slow down, work more slowly. Do not over-reach when working: always retain a stable position. When using the shear to trim a prickly hedge, wear protective gloves.

*Charging the batteries*
Charging the batteries is a simple operation using the battery charger. *Never use this for another appliance.* The batteries can be charged up to five hundred times before they need changing.

Ideally, the air temperature should be about 23 °C. Too low or too high a temperature when charging may damage the cells. When first charging the batteries, after winter storage for example, they may take only eighty per cent of the charge. This is normal, and after several charge-and-discharge cycles, they will return to a one hundred per cent charge.

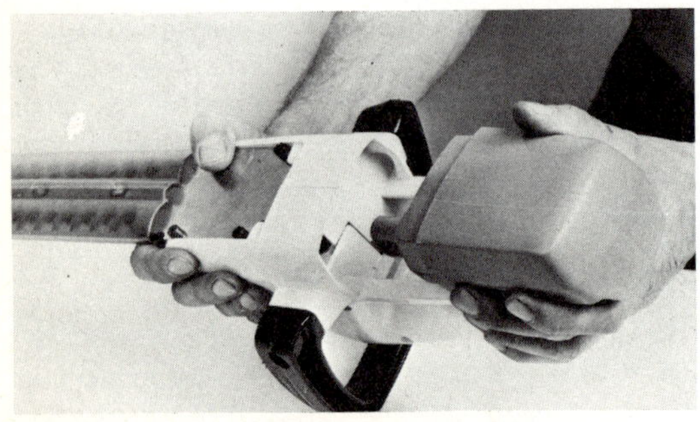

*Hedge trimmer has rechargeable batteries with step-down mains transformer*

Normally recharging takes about twelve hours. During the cutting season the shears can be left on continual charge so that they will be ready for instant use.

## Lawn edge trimmers
Power lawn edge trimmers provide a neat and easy way to finish the edge of a newly mown lawn. However, the edge of the grass must be firm before the edge trimmer can be used. The tool, which again can be mains- or battery-operated, works on a similar principle to the power circular saw, and revolves at 4000 rpm.

The power unit is mounted on the side of the cutting guard, with the assembly supported on a sliding shoe. The unit is guided with a long handle which incorporates an on—off switch and a lock-on button in the pistol-grip handle.

If the cutters become blunt, they too can be sharpened with a file or a carborundum slip or exchanged for resharpened cutters.

## Electric hedge trimmers
An electric hedge trimmer certainly saves time and effort in one of the more time-consuming, repetitive gardening jobs. It has been estimated that the electric tool can cut in ten minutes an area that would take an hour using traditional hand shears.

Moreover, once the technique of using a power cutter has been mastered, the finished effect is often more attractive.

Electric hedge trimmers may be single- or double-edged. Single-edged models are cheaper but will only cut on the forward stroke. This means that if you miss shoots on the first cut, forward progress is stopped while the blade is taken back over the same area.

The advantage of a double-edged trimmer is that, while sweeping forward to make the next stroke, the back-edge blade tidies up any straggling pieces missed on the first sweep.

Additionally, the fact that the shoots of hedge do not grow conveniently in one direction means that when using a single-edged trimmer the shoots that stand up or lie backwards are cut, leaving those that are bent by the cutter uncut. As you can cut only one way, growth then becomes uneven.

The remedy — to cut the hedge in alternate directions — is not easy as it means either turning the trimmer upside down, with the risk of cutting the cable, or leaning over the hedge and cutting from the other side. This problem does not arise with the double-edged trimmer. The blade is swung

*When clipping a hedge, trail the cable safely back over the shoulder*

alternately backwards and forwards, which ensures that all the shoots are trimmed. This encourages thick, even growth.

The cutting performance of the trimmer depends on the length of blade. These are usually between 305 and 610mm long. As the length of the blade determines the speed of the work, choose the blade by the area of hedge to be cut and not the height or width.

### Hedge-cutting attachments

Hedge-cutting attachments can be fitted to your power drill. Two basic types are a 330mm long single-bladed attachment and a 407mm double-edged cutter.

### Fitting

Remove the chuck of the drill and replace this with the standard adaptor used for driving other power tool attachments.

The adaptor fits into a coupling on the attachment which has a cradle to take the body of the drill. There is a retaining clamp with lugs which engages in the front ventilation slot on the gear case.

There are two handles — the pistol grip on the drill and an adjustable, moulded handle fitted on the front of the attachment.

### Mains-operated single-edge 330mm trimmers

There are two Black & Decker single-edge 330mm hedge-trimmer attachments. The least expensive model is not double-insulated and must be run from the mains on a three-core earthed cable.

It has a moulded grip handle which can be screwed into either side of the motor housing. The trimmer cuts at 3000 rpm.

Another model, which is double-insulated, works at 4000 rpm and is fitted with a multi-grip handle.

### Double-edged mains hedge trimmers (407mm and 610mm blades)

The double-edged hedge trimmers are double-insulated and can be run on two-core cable. The larger model is fitted with 15m of two-core cable while the smaller has a short lead and a two-core connector. Both models have large, multi-grip handles.

### Battery-operated, 12V 305mm hedge trimmer

This model can run from a 12V battery or a light-weight battery kit cased and carried in a shoulder sling. Two 6V batteries can be recharged from a mains-operated battery charger.

Another accessory for use with the heavier 12V battery is a trolley which includes a junction box and extension cable to connect to the hedge trimmer.

### Cordless power hedge trimmers

These are more expensive. The battery for the trimmer is housed in the handle and so does away with any cable hazard.

A mains-operated battery charger is supplied with the accessory. The cutting life on each charge would more than outlast the average period spent continuously cutting a hedge.

A fully exhausted battery can be recharged in eighteen hours, the charger having a device to prevent overcharging.

In addition to the double-edged blade, the trimmer has two handles — one moulded on to the top of the housing and one to carry the battery. A key is used to switch the machine on and off. Unless the key is in position the trimmer cannot be switched on.

### Cutting a hedge

The cutting pattern for hedges depends on the type of hedging plants, the time of year, the weather and the desired finished result. Hedges can be encouraged to thicken, grow wider or higher or can be cut back and reshaped.

A hedge should be shaped so that it narrows towards the top. At the end of the season, trim any untidy shoots so that the hedge looks tidy through the winter and new growth starts level in the spring.

While you may be content merely to trim an existing hedge, it is possible to use power trimmers to reshape it. Very tall hedges are difficult to manage and will deprive other plants of light and moisture.

Once shaping has been achieved, the trimmer blade merely removes the new growth at each cutting, stopping at the dense, old wood.

### Trimming

Hedge clippings can be a problem to clear up from grass. This job is made easier if the grass is cut first.

First, and most importantly, make sure that the cord is out of the way. Trim in a direction away from the cable at all times. If you are right-handed keep the cable to your left and cut towards the right. It is a good idea to place the cable over your left shoulder so that at all times it is out of harm's way.

On a straight-sided, flat-topped hedge, trim the sides, first working along one side and back along the other. Then start on the top working from right to left. In this way, there is no chance of fouling the cable.

It is easier to get a neater finish to the cutting edge if the blade is tilted in towards the hedge at a slight angle. This ensures that the growth pointing away from the blade is cut. Reverse the tilt when sweeping back with a double-edged blade.

To avoid gouging out holes in the hedge, sweep the blade forward from the newly trimmed area to the next section to be cut. Start at the left-hand side of the hedge, cutting along the side with upward sweeps of the blade.

The top, whether being cut with a single-edged or a double-edged trimmer, should be worked from right to left, allowing the cutter to sweep over the trimmed area to the next uncut section.

If you are left-handed, merely reverse the cutting directions and do the main trimming with the right-hand edge of the trimmer, looking along the trimmer with the motor on top.

A single-edged cutter will present problems to a left-handed person as the motor and the handle will stick into the hedge instead of being on the outside. The solution is either to use the tool right-handed or invest in a cordless hedge-trimmer attachment.

# Electrical safety and maintenance

There are three categories of power tools: the tool connected to the mains by a three-core cable, the double-insulated tool, which has only two cores (and no earth, just line (live) and neutral), and the battery-operated unit, with a rechargeable battery and battery-charging unit.

Machines with three-core cables have metal cases, which are earthed through the earth cable. Double-insulated tools usually have cases of high-impact plastic, such as Marynal, so that the case cannot become live, and two wires — live and neutral.

The battery-operated unit is perfectly safe; there are no special precautions for use and you do not have the problem of trailing cables. All you have to do is plug the tool into the battery charger when necessary.

Plugs used to connect mains-operated tools should be of the moulded-rubber type and should connect to 13A ring mains or a 15A radial circuit.

The square, three-pin plug is used on ring mains, and the rounded, three-pin 15A plug on radial circuits.

Never plug tools into a conglomerate arrangement consisting of several adaptors.

You may overload the circuit and also provide a poor connection, so that the tool either grinds to a halt or seizes up.

The 13A pattern of plug has a cartridge fuse inside the casing to protect against overload. While usually supplied with a 13A fuse, this should be changed to a 5A fuse.

The live (brown) wire is connected on the right of the plug, beneath the cartridge fuse. The neutral (blue) wire goes to the opposite terminal on the left, and the earth (green/yellow) wire to the top of the plug.

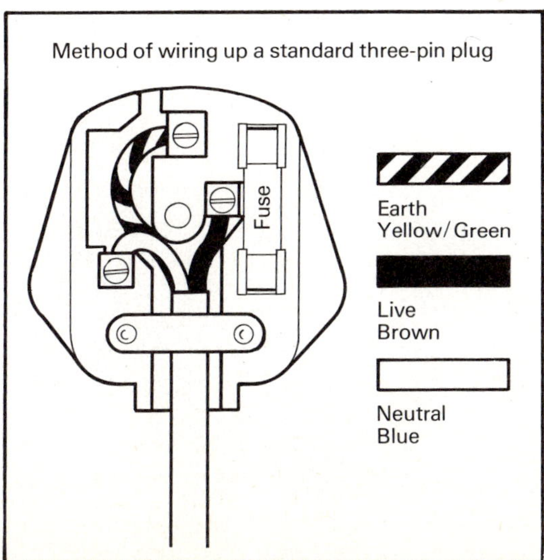


Twist strands tightly together before connecting, and wind these tightly, clockwise around the terminals, making sure that there are no straggly ends, which could cause a short-circuit if they touched other wires. Make sure that the terminals are fully tightened and the cable well clamped in the plug.

Three-wire colour codings are brown — live, blue — neutral and striped yellow and green — earth. Two-wire systems are simply coloured brown and blue.

The cable lead fitted to power tools is generally long enough for most purposes but an extension cable can always be attached, but avoid too much. Your most likely need for extension cable is for use with garden tools, such as lawnmowers and hedge cutters.

Always keep the cable clean, particularly of oil and grease. Do not lift or drag the tool by the cable as this strains the electric connections. Make sure that the cable is never knotted.

Always keep cable on a drum and unwind only as much as you need. Keep cable runs well away from cutting surfaces, and work in a pattern that keeps the cable trailed well behind you when working.

If you do not have a cable drum, you can wind extension cable over the hand and arm in a figure-of-eight fashion, then wind the last turn or so around the middle to hold the cable in place. This will unwind freely in use and will not snag.

Cable drums usually have three-pin sockets set on the side of the drum, to which the cable is connected.

## Connectors
You fit a standard three-pin plug or in-line socket to the other end of the cable to connect to the tool. This plug should be an in-line rubber type when the tool is being used out of doors.

Avoid using connectors to join up runs of cable; try always to use one complete run. Where you have to make connections, such as on to the actual garden tools, use an appropriate two-pin weatherproof rubber in-line connector. These have an arrangement of pins in one half of the plug and sockets in the other half.

The socket should always be connected to the mains — never the pins, which would be live and would give an electric shock if touched.

One half of the connector is flanged, so that it slides partially over the other and

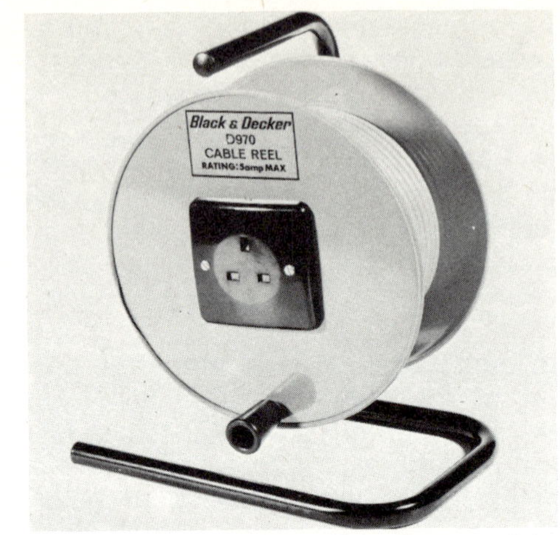

*For safety, to stop tangling, keep cable on drum. Connection is at side*

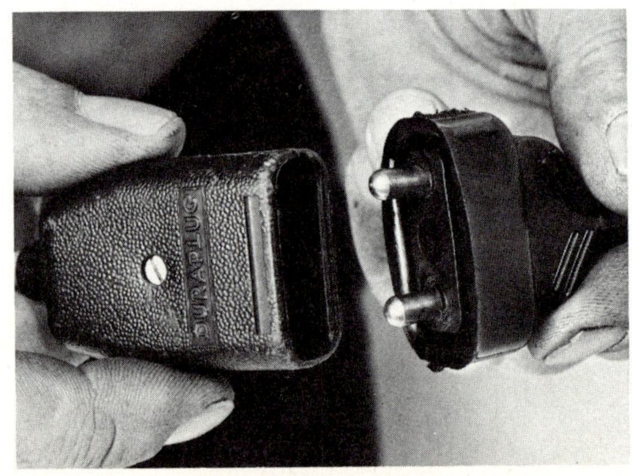

*Always use shrouded, weatherproof plugs for outdoor cable connections*

holds the two halves firmly together.

Some types of moulded rubber socket also contain a fuse in place of the live pin, which plugs into the live socket.

Never disconnect the earth wire on a three-pin connection or extend a three-core cable with a two-core one: you may inadvertently render the casing of the tool live in the event of a fault.

Do not make home-made taped-up joints. These may be poor and ineffective and are likely to pull apart, with possible serious consequences.

All electric cables offer some resistance to the current passing through them, which has the effect of reducing the power available to work the machine.

The principal factors governing the resistance are the length of the cable and the thickness of the wires it contains. A short, thick wire has little resistance while a long, thin wire offers a great deal of resistance.

On average, some sixty metres of two-core extension cable can be used without any serious loss of power. This should be large enough in diameter to carry the current required without too great a drop in voltage, which could impair the performance.

**Ratings chart**

| Amps (indicated on appliance) | 0/2 | 2·1–3·4 | 3·5–5·0 | 5·1–7·0 | 7·1–10 |
|---|---|---|---|---|---|
| Distance (metres) | | | | | |
| 8 | 6 | 10 | 10 | 10 | 18 |
| 15 | 6 | 10 | 10 | 10 | 18 |
| 22 | 10 | 10 | 10 | 10 | 18 |
| 30 | 10 | 10 | 10 | 18 | 18 |
| 60 | 10 | 10 | 18 | 18 | — |
| 90 | 10 | 18 | 18 | — | — |

## Maintenance of double-insulated tools

*Commutator*
Inspect the commutator regularly to ensure that it is clean and free from dirt, oil and grease. Check the solder connections on the leads into the commutator to ensure that none has become loose; then, with the machine running, check that there is no excessive sparking. If either is the case the tool is best returned immediately to a service branch.

*Carbon brushes*
The carbon brushes should be checked frequently to see that they move freely in their guides without sticking and that they make proper contact with the commutator.

The most likely cause of failure or poor performance in a power tool is worn or defective motor brushes. There are two brushes, one on each side of the motor commutator, which are held in by screw-in spring-loaded clips. You can unscrew these clips with a screwdriver to remove the brushes.

Brushes are made of carbon and do eventually wear down, so keeping a spare set is a good idea, particularly if you use power tools a great deal. They should be replaced as soon as they have worn to one-third of their original length, for otherwise serious damage might occur to the armature of the machine. Always use brushes supplied for the make of machine for maximum efficiency.

Dust in the works can cause problems. A buildup of dust inside the body of the drill may lead to the blocking of air vents, resulting in an overheating motor.

Periodically, brush out the ventilation slots with a thin, soft brush with long bristles, then run the motor to displace any accumulated dust.

# Making attachments to walls

There are many devices—in particular, plugs and wall anchors — enabling you to fix shelving and a variety of fitments securely to walls.

Before you drill a hole in a wall, however, you will need to establish the type of surface of the wall, so that you can use the correct drill bit, select the right speed for the drill, and choose the right plug or anchor. Wall surfaces vary between very soft and very hard.

Hard surfaces are drilled with a masonry bit. Metals and synthetic materials are, generally, best drilled using an engineer's high-speed steel twist bit.

Having determined the type of surface with which you are dealing, next make sure that it is safe to drill: find out if there are any buried pipes, cables or other services — and reposition the intended hole if necessary.

Plugs and screws, or bolts in the case of very heavy objects, are used for making fixings into solid walls. Hollow walls, such as plasterboard on timber studding, frequently used in house-wall partitioning for non-load-bearing walls and in ceilings, use cavity-fixing devices.

Always be safe and not sorry; if in doubt,

use a larger fixing. Screws are the usual and best method of securing. Common sizes are no. 8 and no. 12 gauge screws, 25, 30, 50 and 65mm in length.

Although you may be able to pick up a screwdriver attachment for your drill, these are unfortunately no longer easily obtainable. You will need a hand screwdriver — these are gauged to the size of the head of the screw, so choose the right one. Modern screwdrivers have shaped handles, so that you get a better grip and can apply greater torque when tightening the screw.

Solid walls are generally made of brick, concrete aggregate or light-weight cellular building blocks, which offer no special fixing problems.

However, take care when fixing in soft-aggregate materials, since these break up more easily and generally have poorer load-bearing properties than other materials.

Interior linings and finishes differ greatly in construction, strength and thickness. Plasterboard, lath-and-plaster, fibreboard, and synthetic resin compound panels are the most usual.

Linings are usually fixed to a timber framework, called 'studding'. The distances between the timber uprights of stud parti-

tions are called 'centres'; it is into these centres that fixings are usually made, rather than to the actual lining material covering the studs.

Studs usually consist of 75mm × 75mm timber. Distances between studs are usually at about intervals of 380mm. If the framing cannot be used for direct fixing, it is unwise to impose other than the lightest loads.

If possible, fix backing boards to the lining and into the studs and make fixings to these. Use expanding or anchor bolts if you have to fix directly into the lining surface.

**Types of fixing**
The majority of surfaces other than timber need plugging if you are screw-fixing to them.

*Wood plugs*
A hand-shaped wood plug should be cut with a gentle taper to give a tendency to twist and then grip into the surface. Sharp tapers will not, however, fill the recess and may become loose, since wood tends to shrink. The plug can be cut proud of the hole, so that it can be trimmed off afterwards with a sharp knife, to allow for any surface lining, and to ensure a tight fit.

For screw fixings, use hardwood plugs, and drill a small pilot hole, slightly smaller than the screw diameter. Brass or bronze screws should be greased with wax or tallow before being tightened, as they tend to snap in hardwood.

## Preformed plugs

For most uses, preformed plugs — made in fibre, nylon, soft metal and synthetic resin — can be bought almost anywhere. These need only a neat, rounded hole, matched to the plug size, which is just slightly larger than the screw.

Since the holding power of the plug is related to its frictional grip as the screw expands it, it is important that hole, plug and screws should be matched in size. Plugs are numbered to correspond with the screw size and drill.

If, for example, a small screw is used in too large a plug, it will not expand sufficiently to provide a reliable fixing. A large screw used with a small plug will be hard to turn and may jam — and the screw head may be stripped. The screwdriver may also 'cam out' and mar the surrounding surface.

Fibre and soft metal plugs grip the hole and provide a firm fixing. Nylon plugs have teeth or ridges that grip the surrounding surface and prevent the plug from turning.

The size of fibre plugs should be of the

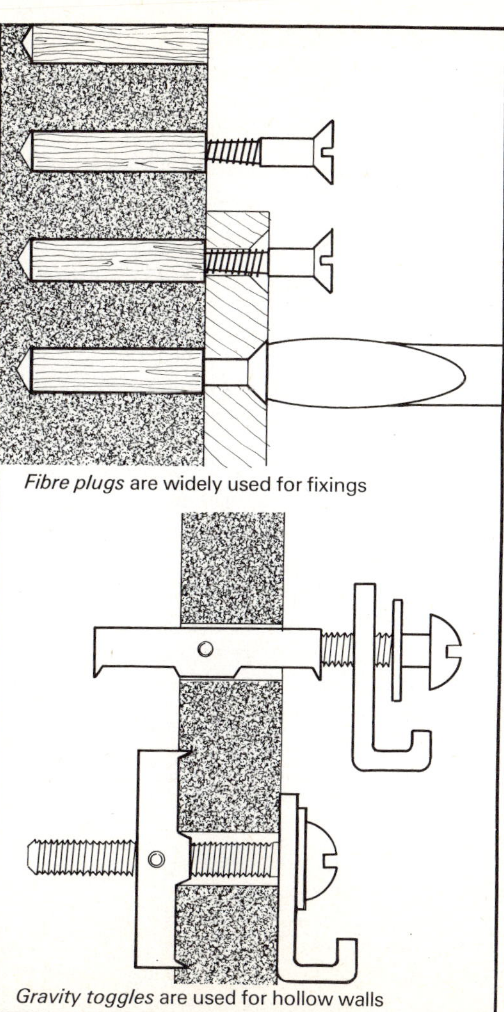

*Fibre plugs* are widely used for fixings

*Gravity toggles* are used for hollow walls

same length or slightly longer than the length of the screw thread, excluding the shank, which should never enter the plug.

## Plastic compounds

Sometimes, particularly in mortar or in soft brickwork, the hole may become excessively enlarged, so the intended screw fixing cannot be made with plugs. Plastic compounds, based on asbestos fibre and cement, can be used for plugging, and you can screw-fix into this. (However, if the hole is very large, it is generally best to reposition it and start again.)

Wet the compound with clean water, form it into a plug of the size required and ram it into the hole. A metal tool is generally supplied with the plastic compound. It is pointed at one end so you can form a pilot hole in the soft compound to start the screw.

If the sides of the hole are parallel, the fixing should be effective. If, however, the hole is wider at the face than at the back, the plug may come out. It is best then to enlarge the hole to a dovetail shape.

Tighten the screw into the moist filler, but if a large mass is used, leave final tightening until the plug has hardened. If there is extreme residual dampness in the area, avoid using a compound.

# Footnote

## Toggles
These are used for fixings in hollow walls.

**Gravity toggles** have a swivel toggle which drops vertically when put through a premade hole in a hollow wall. For heavier fixing, they are used with bolts.

**Spring toggles** have two spring-loaded arms which expand after the toggle is pushed through a hole and grip the inner wall of the fixing. These are also used with bolts for heavier fixing.

**Nylon toggles** are fasteners with a slotted collar which slips over a nylon strip attached to the toggle and are used for screw-fixing.

**Collapsible anchors** stay in place if the screw is removed. Inserting the screw draws metal-gripping shoulders against the inner wall of the fixing.

**Rubber-sleeved anchors** are used for fixing plastic or metal sheets, and can be used in solid walls. The bolt compresses a rubber sleeve against the wall surface.

**Nylon or plastic anchors** ensure that the action of tightening the screw draws the anchor to the wall.

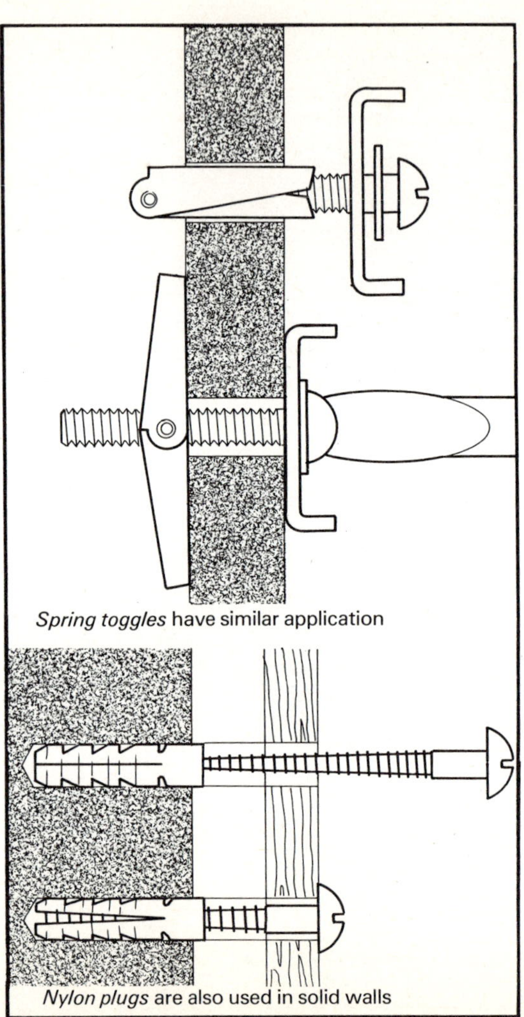

*Spring toggles* have similar application

*Nylon plugs* are also used in solid walls

## Metric
Nearly every country in the world is changing over to the simpler metric system. There is no mystery in metrication. In fact, it is easier to work things out in metric values. Many products, including timber, are now available in metric dimensions.

Many metric sizes or volumes are similar to equivalent imperial ones. Linear measurement is now in millimetres, centimetres (one centimetre equals ten millimetres), and metres (=1000 millimetres). An inch is about 25mm, a foot, 305mm. A metre is just over a yard – 39in. Grams and kilograms (1000 grams) replace the ounce and pound; 25kg represents about 55lb and 50kg, 110lb – about 1cwt. A litre is rather under two pints (1·76 pints). Five litres is about a gallon (1·10 gallons).

# Glossary

This lists most of the tools, attachments and accessories described or illustrated. The choice of drills is particularly wide, offering versatile, sophisticated items at one end and simple, basic ones, for general jobs, including that useful second drill, at the other. The range of accessories is so vast that space does not, unfortunately, allow detailed inclusion by part number. The main products of use in home improvement and repair, woodworking and craft work, are briefly outlined.
The left-hand code identifies the specific Black & Decker product.

## Drills

DN60  Single-speed, 8mm chuck capacity
D500N  Single-speed, 6mm chuck
D420  Two-speed, 6mm chuck
D720  Two-speed, 10mm chuck
D720H  Two-speed, 12mm chuck, plus hammer action
V820  De luxe two-speed, 12mm chuck
V850  De luxe two-speed, 12mm chuck, plus variable control
V860  De luxe variable-speed, 10mm chuck, plus hammer action

## Drill attachments

GD80  Vertical drill stand
D915  De luxe vertical drill stand
D935  Drill stand vice
D980  Horizontal drill stand
D968  Rotary hammer attachment
D976  Right-angle speed changer

## Saws and attachments

DN30  76mm jig saw
DN35  76mm jig saw

DN986  Jig saw attachment
DN55  De luxe 125mm circular saw
HD1000  182mm circular saw (industrial)
D984  Circular saw attachment (125mm)
D985  De luxe 125mm circular saw attachment
D987  De luxe saw bench
D990  Portable saw bench
D992  Saw table

## Finishing tools

DN40  Power finishing sander
D945  Finishing sander attachment
D988  De luxe finishing sander

## Sharpening tools

D370  Bench grinder
D385  De luxe bench grinder
D965  Grinding attachment
DN25  Drill bit sharpener
D998  Disc sanding table
SAG115  Grindermite (industrial tool)

## Specialist tools

D930  Comb-jointing attachment
D932  Multi-purpose woodworking attachment
D933  Milling table
DN65  Router
D994  600mm lathe
D996  Flexible drive shaft (1·15m) attachment
Record 148  Dowelling jig

## Workmate

WM325  Dual-height cast alloy bench
WM525  Dual-height tubular steel bench
WM110  Extender arms
WM120  Metal vice claddings
WM130  Tool tray
WM140  Saw table

D200  Majorvac (vacuum cleaner)
DN100–110  Airless spray gun
7761  Compressor kit

## Accessories

The wide range of accessories includes wood, steel and masonry bits, fixing kits, hole saws, bits for routing and rebating, sanding sheets and sanding discs, in carbide and a variety of grits, rubber backing pads, a range of saw and jig-saw blades, and Xylan-coated saw blades, lambswool bonnet, rag buff, wire cup and disc brushes, paint stirrer, grinding wheels, protective spectacles and face mask.

## Garden tools

D489  Lawnrazor de luxe 300mm cylinder mower
D684  Lawnrazor 300mm low-cost cylinder mower
D689  De luxe 350mm Lawnrazor
D486  De luxe Lawnderette
D484  Lawnderette 300mm light-weight
D485  Lawnderette 300mm with height-of-cut adjustment
D490  Power lawn edger
D473  Power grass trimmer
DNJ454G  Hedge trimmer 600mm ⎱ all three
DNJ452G  Hedge trimmer 400mm ⎰ double-edged
DNJ450G  Hedge trimmer 130mm ⎱ dual action
D450  Economy 130mm hedge trimmer
D892  Double-edged hedge trimmer attachment
D962  Double-edged 600mm super hedge trimmer attachment
D471  Cordless hedge trimmer
D472  Cordless shear
D477  Convertible cordless garden shear
D474  Cordless shrub trimmer

D970  Cable drum

A5098  3·05m cable
D8382  7·60m cable
D8384  15·2m cable